CooL Philosophy

First published in the United Kingdom in 2015 by
Pavilion
1 Gower Street
London
WC1E 6HD

Copyright © Pavilion Books Company Ltd 2015

ISBN 978-1-90939-677-7

A CIP catalogue record for this book is available from the
British Library.

10 9 8 7 6 5 4 3 2 1

Reproduction by Mission Productions Ltd, Hong Kong
Printed and bound by Times Offset (M) Sdn Bhd, Malaysia

This book can be ordered direct from the publisher at
www.pavilionbooks.com

DANIEL TATARSKY

COOL Philosophy

PAVILION

FiLLed with faNTaSTiC Facts FOR KiDs of all Ages

Contents

Welcome to *Cool Philosophy!*

One of my favourite philosophical conundrums is about the chap who bought some socks. This particular fellow was very careful with his money so that when a hole appeared in one of the socks he didn't throw them away but darned them. He was pleased with the result and they looked almost like new. A while later, he noticed another hole. Again, he got out his needle and thread. He really loved these socks and over the course of thirty years holes kept coming and he kept darning. Then one day he looked at his favourite socks and realised they were all darning and no sock. The philosophical question is, are these the same socks that he first bought all those years ago?

Our skin and bones and the materials that make up our physical being are constantly changing and renewing to the point that as you read this book there is nothing left of the original *you* on the day you were born. Like the socks, you have been darned. Are you the same person as the one who was born all those years ago? What makes you the person you are? Is it the physical stuff – the bones, blood and organs all held into shape by your skin and topped off by your hair? Or are you made up of the things you think and say and do?

If you have ever thought 'why did I do that?' or 'what's the point of this?' you're already a philosopher. You don't need to know the answers to these questions, you just need to be sufficiently interested in your life and the lives of others to be asking them.

As with the sock conundrum, a lot of philosophy will have you scratching your head because often there isn't a 'right' answer. In fact that's what's cool about philosophy, nobody can ever say you're wrong.

There have been philosophers since humans first spoke so there's a lot to get through, but take your time with it, give yourself a chance to think things through. It's not about getting to the end so much as making a start.

'Nothing is more active than thought,
for it travels over the universe.'

Thales, the first philosopher

What is Philosophy?

Most areas of study, such as geography, maths or history, are easy to define, but philosophy is more difficult to pin down because it covers so much of everything we do. It's a little like trying to knit fog while wearing boxing gloves...but let's have a go.

Socrates (see page 24) said 'the unexamined life is not worth living', and as a summary of philosophy those seven words are pretty good. Some would say that it is philosophy that separates us from all other living things. It is only humans who ponder what it is to be alive; to be born, live and eventually die.

Descartes (see page 50) went even further than Socrates. His famous statement, 'I think, therefore I am', means that it is thinking that is the one thing that you cannot doubt. The picture is emerging already that philosophy is what makes us human, makes us *us*, and without it we would be as nothing.

Philosophy splits into three main areas; metaphysics, epistemology and ethics. Put simply; what is, what we know and why we do what we do. The funny thing about philosophy is that you can't really study it without actually doing it.

What *is* – this seems obvious until you start to analyse it. A table is a table, but add another piece of wood and it becomes a chair, or take away the legs and it becomes a plank.

We used to 'know' that the Earth was flat, then we discovered it was round. We used to 'know' that everything revolved around the Earth, until we found out that Earth actually travelled round the sun. How do we know that the things we now take for granted will not be overtaken by new knowledge?

Socrates

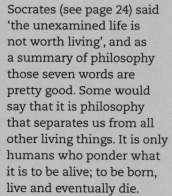

'I cannot teach anybody anything. I can only make them think.'

Socrates was right, of course, and thus the following pages will most likely not teach you a single thing. What they will do, hopefully, is make you think and maybe ask questions that you hadn't even thought about asking before you read the first page of this book. Another of Socrates' wise maxims can help you get off to a good start:

'The only true wisdom is in knowing you know nothing.'

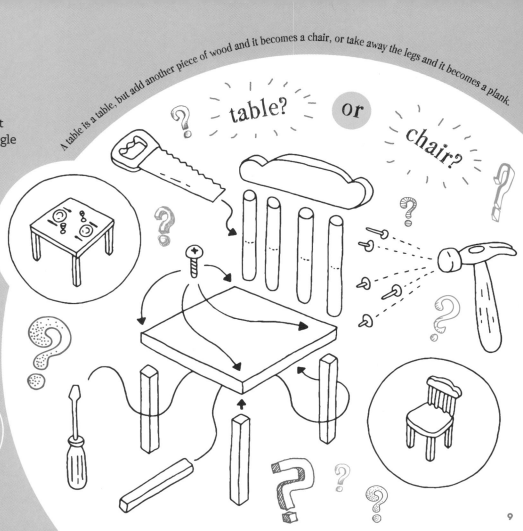

A table is a table, but add another piece of wood and it becomes a chair, or take away the legs and it becomes a plank.

table? or chair?

Philosophy Timeline

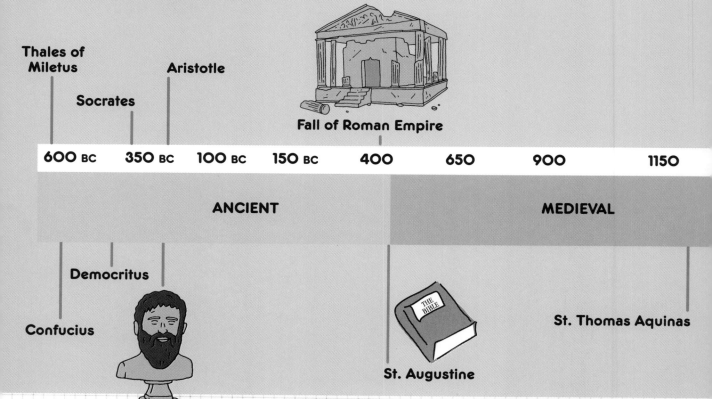

Thales of
Miletus

Socrates

Aristotle

Fall of Roman Empire

| 600 BC | 350 BC | 100 BC | 150 BC | 400 | 650 | 900 | 1150 |

ANCIENT

MEDIEVAL

Democritus

Confucius

Plato

St. Augustine

St. Thomas Aquinas

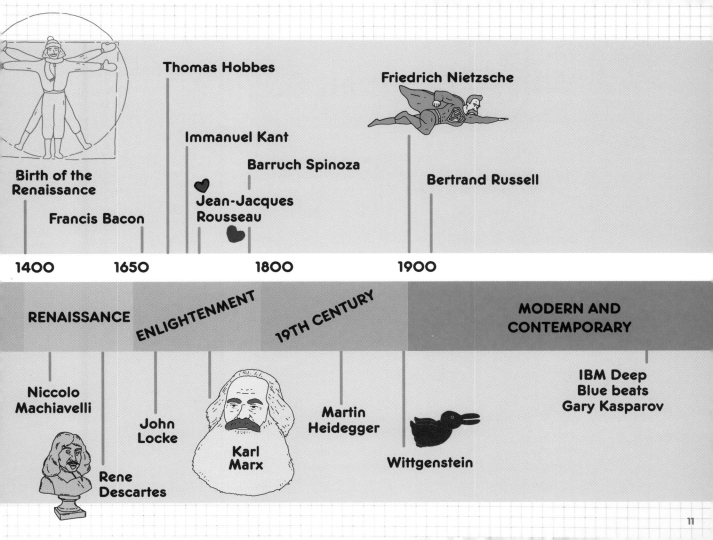

Thomas Hobbes

Immanuel Kant

Barruch Spinoza

Friedrich Nietzsche

Bertrand Russell

Birth of the Renaissance

Jean-Jacques Rousseau

Francis Bacon

| 1400 | 1650 | 1800 | 1900 |

RENAISSANCE

ENLIGHTENMENT

19TH CENTURY

MODERN AND CONTEMPORARY

Niccolo Machiavelli

John Locke

Karl Marx

Martin Heidegger

Wittgenstein

IBM Deep Blue beats Gary Kasparov

Rene Descartes

Where Did it all Begin?
Philosophy in the Ancient World

Without language there could be no philosophy. It is only through the complex communication which language allows that we have been able to develop the great wisdom that is covered in this book.

Having the ability to communicate and think complex thoughts is one thing, but what led to the first great question? For centuries, the only important questions had been 'where is our next meal coming from?' and 'where can I sleep tonight?' We had been a nomadic (roaming) species hunting and gathering, following the food as required, but once we learned how to farm and didn't need to chase food any more, the first permanent settlements sprang up. These were around sources of water and fertile land. Once a settlement was established it would attract further people and grow. With people coming together in permanent settlements, language began to become standardised across great numbers of people.

The birth of permanent settlements should have created a stable existence, but life was still unpredictable. Civilisations sprang up and disappeared, cities came and went, in evolutionary terms pretty quickly. This state of change after a time when it appeared that life and the world were controllable led to the first philosophical question: What is permanent and what is changing?

Everything is changing, all the time. You may go for a swim in the Thames, if you live nearby and are happy to dodge boats, but it's a different river every day. The water's different, the air around it is, even *you're* different.

SOME GREAT PHILOSOPHERS OF THE ANCIENT WORLD

Democritus of Abdera

Socrates of Athens

Plato of Athens

Pythagoras of Samos

Heraclitus of Ephesus

Thales of Miletus

Pyrrho of Elis

ANCIENT GREECE

Leucippus of Miletus

Something to Ponder

Is anything permanent? You'll probably have to start by deciding what permanent means.

'One cannot step twice in the same river.'

Heraclitus

The Pre-Socratics
Water, Water Everywhere

The beauty, and the frustration, of philosophy is that the questions it sets and tries to answer do not have definitive solutions. In maths, 2 plus 2 equals 4, but philosophy is never quite so straightforward.

In answer to that first philosophical question, what is permanent and what is changing, Thales of Miletus chose to consider water. Thales is seen by many as the first Greek philosopher and he is most renowned for his hypothesis that everything is really water. This seems a sensible suggestion for many reasons: water is everywhere, it falls from the sky, it fills the oceans, it's within us and other animals and plants and it can change its form from a gas to a liquid to a solid.

But does this really answer the question or does it merely create another one? When something changes its form is it the same thing? If you take a glass of water and freeze it, can you say that it is the same thing? If it then melts and is heated by the sun until it evaporates and becomes a gas is it still that original glass of water?

So, according to Thales, if I drink a glass of water, the glass and the water are made of the same basic material. As is my hand and mouth and so on. Even the air through which the glass travels to my mouth is made up of water molecules. Truly his world was a place of 'water, water everywhere but not a drop to drink', apart from the water in the glass of course.

Thales' position as the first philosopher is based on more than just his theories on water. He went further by attempting to

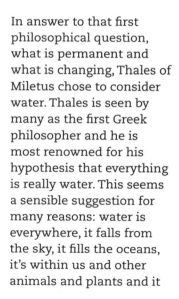

explain natural phenomena by giving rational hypotheses for the events. For instance, he believed that the surface of the Earth floated on water and that earthquakes were the result of roughness in these waters.

'Why, it's nothing at all but pure water!'

Thales' comment on glugging some fine wine.

Five Things You Didn't Know About Thales of Miletus

1 He was the first Greek mathematician

2 He beat Pythagoras to Pythagoras' theory (see page 22)

3 He discovered the cause of solar eclipses

4 On proving his Thales' Theorem he offered an ox to the gods in thanks

5 He may – or may not, depending on who you believe – have been one of the first people to suggest the Earth was a sphere

The Atomic Philosophers
Leucippus and Democritus

The word 'atom', in Greek, means uncuttable and it was this property of what was seen in ancient times as the smallest particle that led Leucippus, Democritus and their followers to put forward their theory of physical atomism. Their idea was that everything was made up of either atoms or the space between those atoms.

Anaxagoras

'There is a share of everything in everything.'

Leucippus

These atoms can form into an unlimited variety of shapes and densities, thus creating everything we are, everything around us, and allowing for the appearance of constant change. The spaces in between, which define the physical world, are absent of any of these atoms, becoming a void. The theory rested on the belief that objects could be infinitely divided to enable anything to be created from them.

In opposition to this theory, Zeno put forward his paradox of Achilles and the tortoise. He believed that infinite divisibility was illogical and came up with one of his trademark paradoxes to expose this (see page 20).

The important thing about Zeno pulling the carpet from under his fellow philosophers is that it marked the beginning of philosophy as a subject where the great thinkers would argue with each other and try to pick holes in each other's ideas. It meant that it had become a subject to be studied and debated.

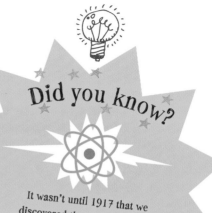

Did you know?

It wasn't until 1917 that we discovered that an atom could be split. Ernest Rutherford is credited with this feat.

Something to Ponder

You receive a yoghurt for your birthday on 1 January. If you eat half of it on your birthday and then half of what's left on 2 January, then half of what's left the next day and so on until it is finished, what date will you finish it? Ignore the use-by date.

The Tao (Way) of Confucius

While Greece was the centre for the foundation of Western philosophy, China was the starting point in the East. Where the West has Socrates, the East has Confucius. His studies and writings focus on the creation or development of the *ideal man*. He believed that man could be taught and improved and even went as far as suggesting that he could be perfected. We're still waiting for that last bit!

Confucius

'The man who moves a mountain begins by carrying away small stones.'

Confucius' teachings come from a secular, non-religious, point of view with a strong focus on the family and self-improvement. So while in the West the early philosophers were trying to answer questions about how and why things existed or people acted as they did, Confucius was more interested in how we could improve the way we were. Many of his most quotable statements are on this topic and you could see a modern job for him in sports psychology:

'Life is simple: we insist on making it complicated.'

'Our greatest glory is not in never failing, but in rising every time we fall.'

There are five pillars which hold up the Confucian belief system; *Rén* (humaneness), *Yì* (righteousness), *Lǐ* (proper behaviour), *Zhì* (wisdom) and *Xìn* (integrity). It is interesting to note that while Confucian thought is non-religious, if you looked at these concepts from a religious point of view they would not feel out of place.

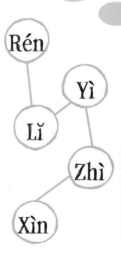

Rén

Yì

Lǐ

Zhì

Xìn

CONFUCIUS TIMELINE

Born 551 BCE → **Aged 3** Confucius' father, a soldier, died → **Aged 19** Married

Aged 50 Became a judge ← **Aged 24** Became a teacher ← **Aged 23** Mother died

Aged 55 Sacked and went back to teaching → **Aged 72** Died

19

Zeno's Paradox

The great early philosophers used their youthful discipline to try to explain and further understand the real world. Zeno turned this all on its head and used the real world to highlight that philosophy was not always a reliable window through which our lives could be observed.

He was born in Elea, in what is now Southern Italy, and is best remembered for his series of paradoxes. In these he took what was accepted thought and used logic to show the absurdity of those beliefs.

In the Arrow Paradox he proves that an arrow in flight is actually motionless. His proof of this is that at any one instant the flying arrow is in a position which would be indistinguishable from a stationary arrow in the same position, therefore, in that instant, the arrow in flight is also stationary.

In his most famous paradox, Achilles and the tortoise, Zeno states that no matter how fast Achilles runs he will never catch the tortoise because by the time he gets to the point where the tortoise was, the tortoise will have moved on to a further point. Zeno was highlighting the absurdity that everything was infinitely divisible.

Something to Ponder
A lot of philosophy involves *thought experiments*, so rather than actually getting a tortoise and a quick runner, try to think this one through. Does the runner catch the tortoise? Are you sure?

Keep up Achilles!

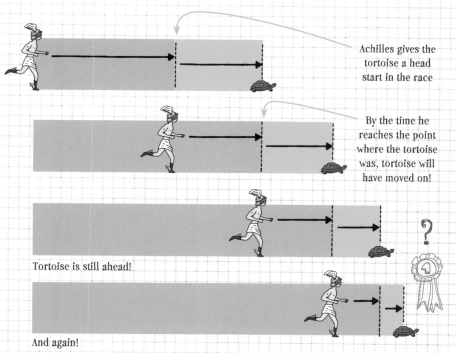

Achilles gives the tortoise a head start in the race

By the time he reaches the point where the tortoise was, tortoise will have moved on!

Tortoise is still ahead!

And again!

Zeno's paradox continues to cause debate to this day. In 1895 Lewis Carroll, best known for *Alice's Adventures in Wonderland*, wrote an article for *Mind*, a journal of philosophy, titled *What the Tortoise Said to Achilles*. It sounds like the start of a joke, but he was attempting to explain the problem in philosophy that arises from explaining a logical principle by having to suggest a previous principle. It begins by surmising that Zeno was wrong and Achilles could have caught the tortoise:

Achilles had overtaken the Tortoise, and had seated himself comfortably on its back. 'So you've got to the end of our race-course?' said the Tortoise. 'Even though it does consist of an infinite series of distances? I thought some wiseacre or another had proved that the thing couldn't be done?'

Pythagoras
Triangles and Beans

Say the name Pythagoras and people will normally think of a triangle; it's a little like how the brand name Hoover has become what we call vacuum cleaners. But ask someone to explain the Pythagorean Theorem and you may be met with a blank stare. He's so strongly connected with geometry and mathematics that it can easily be forgotten how important he was for the development of philosophy.

'There is geometry in the humming of the strings, there is music in the spacing of the spheres.'

Pythagoras

The fact is that for him mathematics was a means to an end and not an end in itself. The end was his philosophy and mathematics was merely a way to get there.

Aristotle, in *Metaphysics*, said: 'the so-called Pythagoreans, who were the first to take up mathematics, not only advanced this study, but also having been brought up on it they thought its principles were the principles of all things.' One example of this was that Pythagoras was the first person to realise that music could be translated into mathematical notation.

The easiest way to understand Pythagoras' Theorem is the diagram on the right. The theory states that in a right-angled triangle the square of the hypotenuse (the longest side) is equal to the sum of the squares of the two other sides.

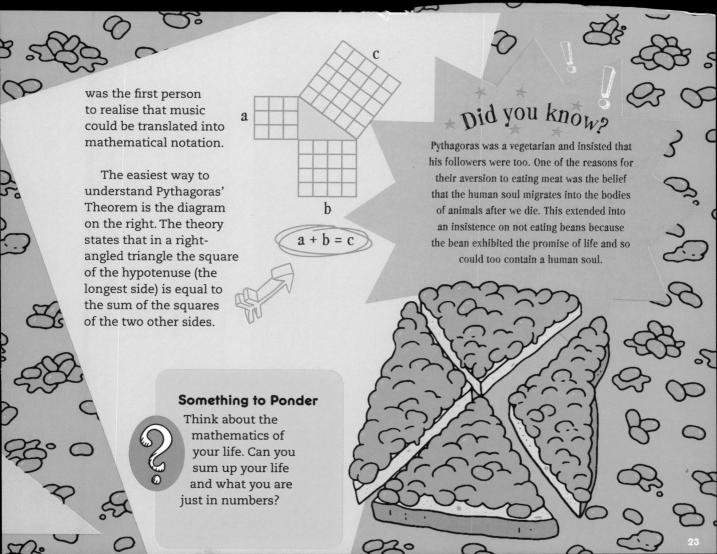

c

a

b

$$a + b = c$$

Something to Ponder

Think about the mathematics of your life. Can you sum up your life and what you are just in numbers?

Socrates What is the Good?

Socrates' father, Sophroniscus, was a stonecutter and initially Socrates followed in his chiselled footsteps. He went on to military service, seeing action with the Athenian army in several campaigns for which his valour was widely recognised. He compared his moral courage later in his life to that which he showed in the battlefield, and expressed surprise that his enemies would expect him to retreat from defeat in debate when he would never have done so in war.

As a philosopher, Socrates was concerned with ethical conduct. His thoughts and teachings attempted to define what was *the good life* – reducing the importance of material things. For Socrates, the good life was a life spent thinking about life, examining the self,

Did you know?

While Socrates (470BC–399BC) is credited as being one of the founders of Western Philosophy he never wrote a single word on the subject. He objected to writing, believing that the act of recording his thoughts would make him less likely to remember them. It is only because his students, Plato and Aristotle among others, reported what he said that we have any record of his ideas. The difficulty with this, known as the Socratic Problem, is that when people report other people's thoughts there is bound to be something lost or changed, either accidentally or deliberately, by the recorder. For example; did he really say: 'Wisdom begins in wonder'? Maybe he actually said: 'Wisdom begins in wander'.

'Beware the barrenness of a busy life.'

Socrates

?

Socrates died by drinking poison!

the inner life. In many ways this was a luxury that led to a life of relative poverty. It's all well and good pondering on your existence but you have to pity his wife, Xanthippe, trying to bring up three sons. You can't put food on the table with a pithy quote.

It has not been recorded what Xanthippe's response was to one such of Socrates' bon mots:

'By all means, marry. If you get a good wife, you'll become happy; if you get a bad one, you'll become a philosopher.'

Something to Ponder

To get you started on the road to becoming a philosopher, have a think about what you did today. Go through all the events, all your random thoughts and actions. When you've finished, ask yourself the question: Do I feel more human?

Plato and the Shadow Puppets of Reality

Much of what we know about Socrates is thanks to the writings of his pupil, Plato. He went on to outshine his teacher but did not totally take away the limelight from the older man. In fact, he used light, and the shadows created by it, to illustrate the central core to his beliefs, as shaped by Socrates, in his _Allegory of the Cave_.

Plato was a mathematician as well as a philosopher; this is becoming a theme. There is clearly a link between the readily definable world of maths and the more fuzzy task of defining the world. Being born into a wealthy family of Athenians may have given him an advantageous start to life but Plato suffered the loss of his father when he was very young. Maybe it was this loss that led him to become such a fierce follower of Socrates. He lays out his own philosophical thoughts in his Socratic dialogues. In these Plato develops arguments through imagined discussions between himself and his teacher. In none of these dialogues does Plato appear himself but instead uses the voice of Socrates, in discussion with a variety of opponents, to eke out the kernel of the issue at hand. But what about those shadows? The allegory involves a cave which is occupied by prisoners whose only view of life is that of shadows cast on the wall by a fire. All they know of life and reality is what they see in these shadows, but they do not know they are just shadows. Plato compares the philosopher to a prisoner who, when freed from the cave, comes to see that what he believed was reality is in fact just a pale imitation of it.

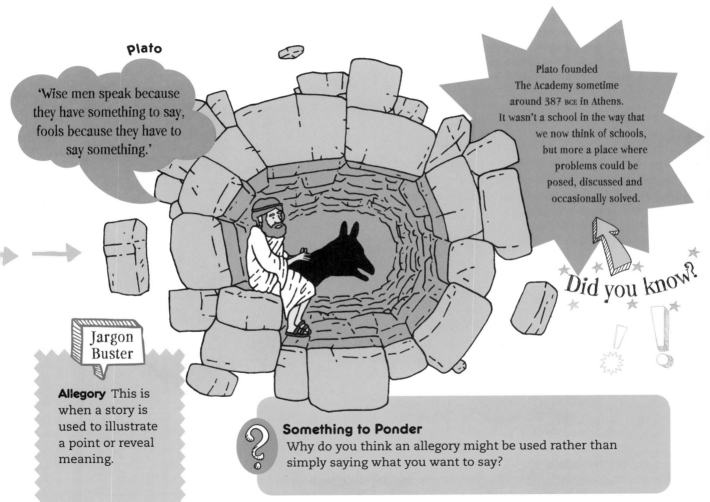

Plato

'Wise men speak because they have something to say, fools because they have to say something.'

Plato founded The Academy sometime around 387 BCE in Athens. It wasn't a school in the way that we now think of schools, but more a place where problems could be posed, discussed and occasionally solved.

Did you know?

Jargon Buster

Allegory This is when a story is used to illustrate a point or reveal meaning.

Something to Ponder
Why do you think an allegory might be used rather than simply saying what you want to say?

The Stoics
Zeno and Epictetus

If Zeno of Citium had held court in his living room or his kitchen a whole movement would have had a different name, but because he gave lectures under a porch, or Stoa, we are now able to celebrate the Stoics.

In the modern, fictional world of the movies, we can find a fictional species who closely resemble the Stoic system in the Vulcans of Star Trek. The best known of these is actually half human, but Spock is renowned for his lack of emotion and reliance on logic. Epictetus, a leading stoic, was born into slavery but was allowed by his master to study philosophy. It is no surprise that with this start to life – his name

translates as 'acquired' – that he was attracted to stoicism. 'Man is disturbed not by things, but by the views he takes of them', he once said.

The stoics believed that you had to defy or deny physical and emotional pain and through this a freedom could be attained. A classic example of this is the Roman soldier Scaevola who, when captured by the Etruscans and threatened with being tortured by

'Whatever!'

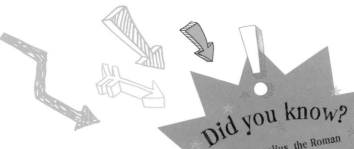

Did you know?

Marcus Aurelius, the Roman Emperor (161–180 AD) was a Stoic and it was his belief in stoicism that made him overcome his indifference to becoming emperor and thus fulfil his duty.

Something to Ponder

We've all been hurt, and normally we'll cry out in pain. It doesn't ease the pain or make it go away so why do we do it? Next time something happens to you, can you imagine yourself not crying out? Would it help you to deal with it?

fire, voluntarily stuck his hand into it. He exclaimed, probably through slightly gritted teeth in spite of his beliefs, that there were a thousand more like him. On seeing this example of Roman, stoic fortitude, his captors surrendered. Can you blame them?

Seneca

'It is the power of the mind to be unconquerable.'

Jargon Buster

Determinism The belief that something that will happen because of a series of events that has happened prior to that event, which make its happening inevitable.

Hmm...Pyrrho the Sceptic and his Pig

A little knowledge is a dangerous thing. It's an old saying, very old indeed. It comes from the ancient Greek philosophers who were collectively known as the sceptics. The sceptics were trying to achieve a state of *ataraxia*, which translates as 'imperturbableness' (if you want to show off) or 'calm' (if you're texting).

Did you know?

Describing someone as a sceptic nowadays is often seen as a negative but Pyrrho, with his ultra-sceptic philosophy, lived to the ripe old age of 90, so he must have been doing something right.

The sceptics fell into two camps: the academics and the Pyrrhonists. The former felt that knowledge was actually impossible. While Socrates had said that the only thing he knew was that he knew nothing, Arcesilaus, a leading academic sceptic, went beyond this. He said that because valid arguments could always be given in favour of two opposing views we could not really know anything for sure.

We couldn't even be sure that we knew nothing.

Pyrrho, on the other hand, was not concerned with whether we could or could not know anything, but was convinced that it was better not to know anything. 'Ignorance is bliss' would sum up his beliefs, and he proved his argument with the story of a pig on a boat in a storm. The passengers, with full knowledge that the storm could sink the boat and that

they could die would be terrified but helpless. The pig was equally as helpless but, and here is what the sceptics based their lives on, would be calm, having no knowledge of an imminent death. If knowledge makes you fearful, how useful is it?

'He [Pyrrho] led a life consistent with his doctrine, going out of his way for nothing, taking no precaution, but facing all risks as they came, whether carts, dogs or precipices...'

Diogenes Laertius (*Life Of Pyrrho*)

Something to Ponder
Would the greatest gift you could have be to know your future, or is the greatest gift not knowing what life holds?

Something Else to Ponder
The modern meaning of sceptic is a person who questions accepted opinion, whereas in ancient philosophy a sceptic denies the possibility of knowledge. Ponder the journey from the latter meaning to the former.

Aristotle's Missing Basketball

There's a painting by Raphael called *The School of Athens*. This fresco decorates one of the walls in the Vatican and represents philosophy, showing many of the best-known thinkers of Ancient Greece. Right in the middle of the piece you can see Plato with one of his pupils; Aristotle.

The older man's right hand is held vertically with the index finger pointing straight up, while his student's right hand is held forward, with the palm flat and perpendicular to the ground. Scholarly jokers with a sporting bent have suggested that they have lost their basketballs – Plato's would have been spinning on his finger,

'All men by nature desire to know. An indication of this is the delight we take in our senses; for even apart from their usefulness they are loved for themselves.'

Aristotle

while Aristotle would have been bouncing his on the ground.

Was Raphael trying to show their different styles of shooting hoops? Of course not, but he was indicating how their philosophies differed. Plato, pointing to the sky and ideal forms, and Aristotle affirming that the truth of reality lay on the ground, in the physical world around us. He was as much a biologist as a philosopher.

Aristotle's theories on natural science survived him by two thousand years, with his thoughts either not being dispelled or still holding true after all that time.

Every S is P · one or both false · No S is P

S P · S P

true · false · contradictory · true · false

S P · one or both true · S P

Some S is P · Some S is not P

Jargon Buster

Aristotle is credited with creating 'syllogism' as a form of logic but what is it? **Syllogism** is when a conclusion is drawn from two statements which share a term with the conclusion and a term with each other which is not in the conclusion. Get it? No? Here's an example:

Socrates is a man. All men are mortal. Therefore Socrates is mortal.

Something to Ponder
Can you come up with your own syllogism?

The Fall of Rome and the Beginning of Medieval Philosophy

Rome wasn't built in a day and the fall of the Roman Empire did not happen overnight: it gradually descended, declined and disappeared over three hundred years from the third to the fifth century, give or a take a day or so. The effect on philosophy was profound because, nature hating a vacuum, the gap left by the fallen empire was taken by the Barbarians.

It was the Barbarians who filled the gap, and what makes this important for philosophy is that the world became a bit more messy. The strict rules imposed by the Empire disappeared, as did many of those incredibly long straight roads. For a thousand years philosophical thought was sent underground as the only scholars left were religious ones and they took refuge in monasteries. This meant that almost all of medieval philosophy is concerned with proving the existence of God.

Barbarians translates as 'non-Greek' and they came from pretty much everywhere and were not one generic group. With none of them having a written language in their culture, the descriptions of them come from the Romans, who lumped them into one group, Not Us. There were the Huns, the Goths, the Visigoths, the Vandals, the Angles, the Saxons, and the Franks. Can you place them on a map?

'There are three attributes for which I am grateful to Fortune: that I was born, first, human and not animal; second, man and not woman; and third, Greek and not barbarian.'

Thales

Another, perhaps more modern, definition of barbarian is that of an uncultured person: someone without learning and without the desire to use the enquiring mind. It is no surprise then, that this was a fallow period for any philosophy beyond the religious.

The Problem of Evil
Saint Augustine and the City of God

Saint Augustine (354–430) was one of the first Christian philosophers. His writings have been highly influential in Western and Christian philosophy. Interestingly he wasn't born into Christianity but converted in his thirties upon reading the section of the Bible often referred to as the 'transformation of believers'. As is often the case with someone who chooses his path, he was more passionate than many of those born into it.

His greatest obsession was the difficulty of trying to reconcile his love of God with the existence of evil. The specific problem being the syllogism that if God created everything and evil exists then God must have created evil.

His explanation for it is that God did not create evil, but in giving us free will he allowed for us to choose not to be good. Thus evil is not a thing in itself but is a lack of goodness. And if evil is not a thing then it is still true to say that God created everything but not evil. Very neat and tidy.

Two quotes from Saint Augustine shed further light on his beliefs:

Something to Ponder

Alan and Ben are both good runners. They enter their village's annual running race and both really want to win. In wanting themselves to win they are, in effect, wishing that the other loses. Does this make them bad people? Would it be okay, in God's eyes, to pray for the win?

'The world is a dangerous place to live; not because of the people who are evil, but because of the people who don't do anything about it.'

Albert Einstein

Boo!

'It was pride that changed angels into devils; it is humility that makes men as angels.'

'Seek not to understand that you may believe, but believe that you may understand.'

Is this syllogism valid?

- God created everything
- Evil exists
- God must have created evil

Can you think of a syllogism that still acknowledges that God created everything but also makes it clear that evil is not among those things?

Hiss!

37

Does God Exist?

One of the greatest philosophical questions is 'Does God exist?' One of the reasons it is such a great question is that it is impossible one way or the other to prove it. It is true to say this of most of the ongoing debates – the thing which makes them ongoing is that the answer is not provable.

Thomas Aquinas came up with five arguments with which, he thought, the existence of God can be proved. These have become known as *The Five Ways*.

Thomas Aquinas

'To one who has faith, no explanation is necessary. To one without faith, no explanation is possible.'

① Argument from Motion

Everything that moves must have been propelled by something else, but the sequence cannot go on forever so there must be a first mover. That mover is God.

② Argument from Efficient Cause

Things are caused in the world but nothing can exist prior to itself, therefore if the first thing in a sequence does not exist, neither does the sequence. This cannot go on forever, otherwise nothing would exist so there must be a first thing; God.

Something to Ponder
One of the problems with accepting God's existence is that you can't see him (or her, if that's more to your liking). Think of some other things that you cannot see but which you believe in, or don't.

3 **Argument of Necessity** Everything that exists did at one time not exist. There could have therefore been a time when nothing existed. It is absurd to think of nothing existing, so there must have been a thing in existence upon which everything else is dependent; this is God.

4 **Argument from Gradation**
All things can be compared for their qualities and there must be perfection at one end of this continuum; this is God.

5 **Argument from Design**
Things happen for a reason, or are guided. For the world to be in existence it had to have been designed, and that architect is God.

The Renaissance and the Rediscovery of the Human

The Dark Ages, which had been brought on by the spread of the Barbarians, were coming to an end by the 14th century. The Renaissance, which means 'rebirth', began in Italy (which makes it surprising that it is not more commonly known by the Italian name *Rinascimento* rather than the French) and spread throughout Europe. The use of paper and the invention of the printing press aided this movement, as it was much easier to distribute the new learning. Imagine what would have happened if they'd had the internet?

Petrarch

'Man has no greater enemy than himself.'

The Renaissance concerned all the elements of life from the arts and sciences through to trade and technology, but as far as philosophy was concerned it created a sort of back-to-the-future in thinking. Ancient texts were revisited and translated, ancient as in pre-Christianity, and a belief was developed that eloquence and the use of language was key to our humanity and intellectual growth. In this move away from Christian philosophy there was a shift in focus from what would become of us in the next world to concentrating on what we were experiencing now.

This movement is known as humanism and puts the emphasis on what it is to be a human being. It was a humanist, Petrarch, who first coined the phrase *The Dark Ages* to describe what had come before the Renaissance.

The quintessential Renaissance man is Leonardo da Vinci, master of all trades from art through to science. A renowned sculptor, he also invented the helicopter. He

'The noblest pleasure is the joy of understanding.'

Leonardo da Vinci

The Vitruvian Man...

Da Vinci's Top Five Achievements

1 Mona Lisa The most famous painting ever

2 The Last Supper The most famous mural ever.

3 The Vitruvian Man The most famous combination of art and geometry

4 The Parachute Centuries ahead of its time

5 Anatomical studies

...or is he inventing a snow angel?

Leonardo da Vinci

'Simplicity is the ultimate sophistication.'

was ahead of his time and so never saw it fly but it proved that there was little he could not do. He wasn't really known as a philosopher, but it's impossible to ignore him when considering this period.

Machiavelli and the Craft of Politics

Having a human trait named after you is a sure sign that you have entered the legend of great philosophers, and one such man is Niccolo Machiavelli (1469–1527). To be Machiavellian is to be cunning, double-dealing or two-faced. They say there's no such thing as bad publicity, but in a way this is a shame for Machiavelli as he was not himself like this but simply exposed this sort of behaviour in his book, *The Prince*.

'It is much safer to be feared than loved because...love is preserved by the link of obligation which, owing to the baseness of men, is broken at every opportunity for their advantage; but fear preserves you by a dread of punishment which never fails.'

Machiavelli, *The Prince* (1532)

MACHIAVELLI TIMELINE

1469
Born in Florence, Italy

1498
Takes role as the second chancellor of the republic

1498
Elected defence/war Secretary

1501
Marries

1512
Sacked from the chancery

1513
Tried for conspiracy

1513
Writes *The Prince*

1521
The Art of War is published

1527
Dies in Florence, Italy

He was a humanist but having been, wrongly in his belief, kicked out of political office and tortured for supposed conspiracy, he felt mankind had fallen and his view of his fellow man was pessimistic. These feelings were explored and expanded upon in *The Prince*, in which he suggested that to be a successful politician it was better to be feared than loved. This was not necessarily how he wanted to be but was the behaviour he had seen among politicians who succeeded. Rulers should not seek to be admired but should strive only to maintain power, he suggested.

Something Else to Ponder

What is the job of a politician? Is it to rule or is it to make sure they get re-elected? Are effective rulers 'good'?

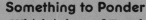

Something to Ponder

Which is better? To rule by fear, having people do things because they are afraid of the consequences of getting it wrong? Or to rule by love, having people do things because they want to please you?

Montaigne the Sceptic

'My life has been full of terrible misfortunes, most of which never happened.'

Michel de Montaigne's motto was 'What do I know?', or as he said it 'Que sais-je?' Yes, he was French. His philosophical thought sought a new engagement with classical scepticism as the serene life that he had known was being shattered by the religious wars all around him in 16th century France.

Did you know?

Montaigne suffered from kidney stones, and while these were painful and caused him a lot of suffering he did not shy away from them in his musings. He even went so far as to record the size and shape of the stones he managed to pass.

His philosophical life was not worked out in debate with others but in quiet solitary contemplation in a tower, which formed one of the corners of his chateau in the Dordogne. He wrote hundreds of essays, which were published in the plainly entitled *Essais* in 1580. *Essais* in this case translates as 'tests', 'attempts' or 'tastings'. His writings were, in essence, a diary of his thoughts and actions in which he examined, in sometimes microscopic detail, the everyday events which, when accumulated, make up what we call a life. These incidents were then the springboard for a greater examination of what it is to be human.

It is interesting to note that Montaigne's navel-gazing style of philosophy was looked down on at the time of his writing and yet it falls very much in line with Socrates' belief that we must examine our lives. Montaigne was, as shown in his essays, one of the first philosophers to suggest that humans are not the only creatures with an inner life. One of his most famous quotes

'When I am playing with my cat, how do I know that she is not playing with me?'

Fetch!

asks whether cats have more fun playing with us than we do with them. He even ridiculed people who put themselves above other animal life, and was centuries ahead of his time in his concern with the sufferings of animals.

Something to Ponder

Have you played with a cat? If we say that 'yes, the cat is playing with me', what do you think the cat is thinking?

Francis Bacon's Frozen Chicken

Sir Francis Bacon (1561–1626) ripped up the philosophy rulebook, chucked it away and started again. If renaissance was a rebirth, then Bacon's effect on philosophy could see him being called the midwife to the scientific revolution.

'Ipsa scientia potestas est.' – Knowledge itself is power.

Francis Bacon, *Meditations Sacrae and Human Philosophy*

Like Machiavelli before him, Bacon didn't set out to be a philosopher. Unlike the ancient Greeks there wasn't the luxury of simply sitting around thinking about things, and his early life saw him operating in politics when he was elected as an MP at the early age of 20. He remained in public service until his early sixties. Whereas Machiavelli waited until after his working life was over, Bacon was writing all the way through.

Possibly his greatest contribution was his collection of scientific works in which, over five volumes, he put forward his ideas for the total rethinking of scientific methods and how these can be used to improve our lot.

At the core of Bacon's philosophy was a belief that data should be collected in a methodical way based on close observation of nature. Hypotheses could then be suggested, tested and proved against this data. This is known as induction.

He clearly had an enquiring mind and some believe it was this which led to his death. Curiosity killed the cat, but Bacon's bacon was cooked by an uncooked chicken. He was travelling in Highgate, North London, on a snowy day when he suddenly had the idea that

Something to Ponder
Bacon believed that observation and collection of data was the start of all science and philosophy. Find something to observe, collect the data on it and then, this is the tricky bit, come up with a theory.

Did you know?

Bacon's political career saw him careering (sorry) around the country as he represented seats all over the country – starting with Bossiney in Devon. From there he went to Weymouth and Melcombe Regis, Taunton, Liverpool, Middlesex, Ipswich and finally Cambridge University.

the snow could preserve meat. He stopped the carriage, bought a chicken and stuffed it with snow. Within three days he was dead. Officially he died of pneumonia but he could equally have contracted an infection from the chicken. There is no record of what happened to the bird.

Nasty, Brutish and Short
The World of Thomas Hobbes

The social contract is something that almost every person has signed but not with a pen on a piece of paper. Simply by choosing to live within an ordered society we have all agreed to follow certain rules and agreed to be bound by them. The journey to this situation was an organic thing and happened by minute degrees over centuries. Thomas Hobbes was one of the first people to recognise that this was the corner into which we had painted ourselves – or the solid foundation on which our lives are built, depending on how you look at it.

'It is not wisdom but Authority that makes a law.'

Thomas Hobbes

nasty

short

brutish

Hobbes was born prematurely, in April 1588, and came to believe that his arrival had been hastened by his mother's fear on hearing of the advance of the Spanish Armada. This fostered in him a fear of war...

'Whatsoever therefore is consequent to a time of war, where every man is enemy to every man, the same consequent to the time wherein men live without other security than what their own strength and their own invention shall furnish them withal. In such condition there is no place for industry... no knowledge of the face of the earth; no account of time; no arts; no letters; no society; and which is worst of all, continual fear, and danger of violent death; and the life of man, solitary, poor, nasty, brutish, and short.'

Thomas Hobbes

Something to Ponder

Think about your house, and imagine that it is a country. You are the ruling authority and your immediate neighbours are the citizens. Have you signed up to a social contract? Does it work? Is it fair? Is it fair to both sides? What would you change about it?

This fear encouraged him to seek ways of avoiding war, which he laid out in his great work, *Leviathan*. In it he recognises the social contract but emphasises the need for a dominant authority to make sure the contract is upheld. In some ways his philosophy contains a paradox, on the one hand he champions the rights of the individual but on the other he believes that to maintain order there needs to be a strong ruling authority.

Descartes 'I think, therefore I am' →

René Descartes' discussions on life totally ignore everything that had gone before. Whereas most philosophers take as their starting point previous arguments and either go further or contradict them, his stated aim was to give himself a blank piece of paper with no beginning other than his own ideas. That doesn't mean to say that what he subsequently came up with was totally original, but it meant that he was not influenced by past works.

He's best remembered for just three words, '*Cogito ergo Sum*'. Actually, when translated it's five words, 'I think, therefore I am', but what did he actually mean by this? It would be possible to argue that he was simply expanding on Socrates' '*the unexamined life is not worth living*', but there is much more to what he is saying. He worked with what he called a 'method of doubt', doubting everything he knew and saw, even entertaining the idea of an 'evil demon' deceiving him all the time; such that, in the end the only thing he could be sure of was that he did exist in spite of his doubt, because in order to doubt he had to be thinking, and in order to be thinking he had to exist.

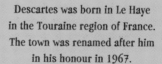

Did you know?

Descartes was born in Le Haye in the Touraine region of France. The town was renamed after him in his honour in 1967.

'If you would be a real seeker after truth, it is necessary that at least once in your life you doubt, as far as possible, all things.'

Descartes

Something to Ponder

We perceive life through our senses, but because we don't exist outside of these senses how do we know that the stimulus we are receiving are the things that we perceive them to be or simply illusions of those things? The film *The Matrix* uses this concept. The characters think they are living in the real world but in fact their senses are being tricked by the computer feed straight into their brains. A simpler example of this is when you see a stick half submerged in some water. It appears to be bent at the point it enters the water. Until you take the stick out of the water you do not know if it is bent or straight. Can you think of other things, not just visual, where your senses can be tricked?

The Mind-Body Problem

The mind-body problem is one which is still vexing philosophers and has done ever since Descartes formulated the debate. In his view the mind and the body are two separate substances which, when they work together form a fully functioning human but which could equally function totally separately.

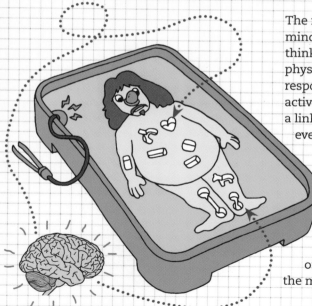

The mental entity, the mind, is involved with thinking, while the physical entity, the body, is responsible for the physical activity. There is of course a link between the two and even an interdependence. The link being that it is the mind which sends signals to the body to make it do things, but some of these signals are only invoked because of information which the mind receives from the body. Take, for example, the need to visit the loo. The physical body registers that the bladder is full and sends a signal to the brain that this is the case. The mind processes this information and makes a decision on what should be done about it. In most cases, we hope, that involves finding a lavatory and doing the necessary. It's when this symbiotic relationship breaks down that accidents occur. For example, drinking too much alcohol dulls the senses and the important message is delayed...but let's not go there!

The problem, though, stems from the fact that one substance (the mind) is stored somewhere within the other (the body). The obvious thing to suggest is that the mind is in the brain – but where in the brain and is the mind really just in the brain? If you stub your toe, you feel the pain at the site of the stubbing, not in your brain, so is the mind all over our body? If your toe is stubbed badly and has to be amputated, do you then lose some of your mind? Probably not.

The world is a physical place: if every substance disappeared, there would be no bodies and there would be no minds. This would imply that the mind cannot survive without the body, but can the body survive without the mind?

What is the mind, then? Is it simply the output from a billion electrical impulses in our bodies and brains? If it is just this, why could it not be created artificially? What makes the mind unique in each of us and how do we know that the way we perceive the world is the same as our neighbour?

Something to Ponder

If the mind is separate from the body but needs the body to function, how much of your body do you need to keep to still have a mind? We know you can lose all of your limbs and still think, but how much more of your body could be lost? It's a grisly thought, but could you survive as just a brain kept alive in a chemical vat?

> ### Jargon Buster
>
> **Dualism** The theory that the mind and the body are two distinct things.
>
> **Monism** The theory that the mind and the body are one.

The Blank Slate of John Locke

John Locke saw the mind at birth as we might see a clean blackboard; totally blank. Everything we know, everything we learn and deduce from what we know is written on that blackboard by the chalk of experience.

Over the four books which make up *An Essay Concerning Human Understanding* (1690), Locke developed his theory which would become one of the main contributions to the philosophical school known as 'empiricism'.

Book 3 looks at language and how man has attributed meaning to different sounds which then allows him to develop complex notions about himself and the world around him.

Book 1 sets out his argument for us all starting off with a blank slate, that there are no innate principles. This flies in the face of Plato, who would have it that we are born with all our ideas and as we go through life we simply learn to understand them better.

Book 2 looks at how we then acquire our principles through experience. This is either by actual sensory perception and/ or by reflecting on our minds and the ideas therein.

Book 4 is a general look at knowledge and how it is the result of the thoughts and experiences we have had.

'No man's knowledge here can go beyond experience.'

Locke distinguishes between Primary and Secondary qualities in the things we experience. The primary are to do with form; shape, size and so on, while the secondary relate to how the things make us feel or the effect they have on us. So the primary qualities of a table are its dimensions, while the secondary would be the colour of the wood, the hardness of it, the smell it might give off. This is interesting when we think about our own mind. We can establish, by thought, the secondary qualities of it but it has no primary qualities.

Something to Ponder
Traditionally there are five senses: sight, touch, taste, smell, hearing. Can you experience things without these? What are they? Does that mean there are more than five senses? Would philosophy have developed differently if our main sense was smell? (I stink, therefore I am).

Jargon Buster

Empiricism
The theory that all knowledge is gleaned from information experienced by the senses.

WOW! That's a lot of experience!

John Locke

'Parents wonder why the streams are bitter, when they themselves poison the fountain.'

The Rationalists Spinoza and Liebniz

Sitting on a comfortable chair in a room, with no windows or doors, maybe just a little light, was sufficient, so the rationalists believed, to put you in a position to gain knowledge. Simply pondering was enough, they said. It was not necessary to experience things in order to understand and make sense of them.

Baruch Spinoza and Gottfried Liebniz were rationalists, which means that they believed that the truth could be found just by thinking; it was not necessary to have the sensory stimuli or experience in order to learn. For instance, they would say that if you hit something hard with your hand, it will cause you pain, this you know. You don't need to do it to know it. While this example seems obvious for something so physically straightforward,

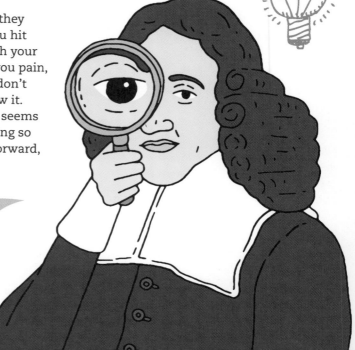

Baruch Spinoza

'The highest activity a human being can attain is learning for understanding, because to understand is to be free.'

Gottfried Liebniz

'There are also two kinds of truths: truth of reasoning and truths of fact. Truths of reasoning are necessary and their opposite is impossible; those of fact are contingent and their opposite is possible.'

Baruch Spinoza earned his living as a glass grinder, his work on rationalism was merely a side-line. Sadly, his main occupation brought him an early death as he died from lung disease caused by inhaling glass dust, aged 44 in 1677.

Did you know?

Jargon Buster

Axiom A statement which is accepted as self-evidently true.

they applied the same method to all of their philosophy.

Much of Spinoza's thinking is laid out in *Ethics* which was published after his death. His starting point is a list of axioms such as 'The knowledge of an effect depends on and involves the knowledge of a cause.' He then goes on to validate these.

While being one of the 17th century's greatest thinkers, Leibniz is also well known for his invention of mechanical calculators such as his Leibniz wheel.

Is This a Dagger I See Before Me? Rationalism Versus Empiricism

It's not quite The Rumble in the Jungle but the ongoing debate between rationalists and empiricists is no less ferociously fought, it's just that they use their minds rather than their fists.

ding ding!

In the red corner is Empiricism: in order to learn about something you have to experience it. To fully understand the pain of a punch in the face, someone has to punch me in the face.

In the blue corner, and totally unprepared

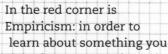

EMPIRICISM

to throw or receive a real punch, are the Rationalists, sitting on their stool, imagining the punch coming towards them, seeing it in their mind's eye, feeling the force of leather on cheek and how it knocks their head back, bouncing their brain off the inside of their skull.

One of the classic ways to prove an argument or your point of view is not to

concentrate on your side but to disprove the opposite viewpoint. So how does that work in this classic confrontation?

'There is nothing either good or bad but thinking makes it so.'

William Shakespeare

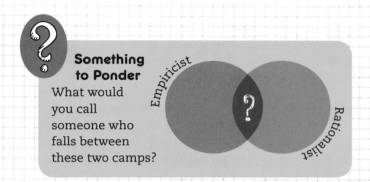
'All our knowledge begins with the senses, proceeds then to the understanding, and ends with reason. There is nothing higher than reason.'

Immanuel Kant,
Critique of Pure Reason

A rationalist would say that empiricism does not work because you cannot trust your senses. The stimuli may be false, or create an incorrect reaction in your senses. We've all sat on a train and believed it to be moving because the one next to us has moved.

Getting up from that knockdown, an empiricist would suggest that without cause there is no effect.

Something must happen for something else to happen. The 'innate knowledge' that forms the basis of all rationalist arguments simply does not exist without the initial stimuli.

There is a case for saying that, as with the mind-body problem, one could not exist without the other. Knowledge is gained by the empiricist but is filtered through a

rationalist's prism. Equally the rationalist's wanderings are all well and good but without the filter of experience they are nothing more than smoke in the wind.

RATIONALISM

To Be Is To Be Perceived
George Berkeley's Zen-like Subjective Idealism

George Berkeley (1685–1753) was, like John Locke, an empiricist, but he saw a problem with his predecessors' thinking. Yes, our ideas come from our observations, but how do we know that the things we are observing actually exist out there, beyond ourselves? As it is impossible to be outside of yourself you cannot, reckoned Berkeley, see if your perceptions are real.

Something to Ponder
You can't see beyond the horizon and yet you never fall off the end. Is that which is just beyond the horizon there before you can see it, or does it come in to existence at just that moment when you perceive it?

To overcome this problem, Berkeley developed the idea that there is no *out there*, in effect that matter does not exist beyond our perception of it and if we don't perceive something then it is not there.

'Esse is percipi.'
– To be is to be perceived.

Out of this thought came his most remembered observation regarding a falling tree in a forest. If it falls, he suggested, but no one is there to observe its falling, it would not make a sound. In fact, he went on, it wouldn't even fall, actually it wouldn't even exist and neither would the forest in which it fell.

Objects then, for Berkeley, were merely

an accumulation of perceptions for which we have come up with names to identify them. You only call a chair a chair because someone has told you that the object you are sitting on is called a chair. Berkeley's stance is called *idealism*; that we can only access the world via the perception given to us of it by the mind, in essence it gives us the idea.

Did You Know?
Berkeley in California is named after this philosopher from Ireland, although they pronounce it differently stateside. This shouldn't be of concern, for if we don't hear them pronouncing it *wrongly* they aren't actually doing so and indeed don't even exist!

Shhh!

Are we really here?

Black Swans and David Hume

David Hume was born in Edinburgh in 1711 and died there in 1776. Would it thus be valid to say that he spent his whole life in Edinburgh?

The example of taking a limited number of observations and then making an assumption based on them is called *inductive reasoning* and Hume was one of the first people to ask the question of whether it is valid to do so.

The subject is important because it forms the foundations of Hume's world-view. Hume noticed that we assume that nature will continue along its regular path; for example, if all the swans we have ever observed are white then all swans that we will see in the future will also be white. He was not happy with this conclusion as he believed that at some point a black swan would emerge.

'I haven't seen any black swans round here – have you?'

The only way then that inductive reasoning can be utilised is to allow for uncertainty and have this uncertainty regulated by our gut feeling or instinct. So while we may never have seen a black swan and we can be pretty certain that the next swan which swims into view will be white, we are also not sent into a tailspin if we do happen upon a black swan.

David Hume

'A wise man proportions his belief to the evidence.'

Jargon Buster

Induction The reaching of general principles from specific observations.

Deduction The reaching of a particular instance from general principles.

Something to Ponder

Should we also consider the possibility of a brown swan? A black and white swan? A purple one? Where does it end?

Something Else to Ponder

Police work involves a lot of deduction. Sherlock Holmes and Hercule Poirot are always deducing this or that based on clues. Why do you think we never hear of them inducing anything?

The Enlightenment and the Clockwork Universe

'Gravity explains the motions of the planets, but it cannot explain who sets the planets in motion.'

Isaac Newton

The Age of Enlightenment, which covered the late 17th and 18th centuries, was, as the name suggests, a time when people's eyes were opened to a new way of thinking; a way that opposed superstition and myth, and was based purely on a set of principles using experimentation and observation to test those principles and revising them according to the results. Foremost among the 'enlightened' was Isaac Newton and his Laws of Motion.

These laws, along with his law of gravitation, gave a solid framework within which the world and even the universe could be explained. It even gave rise to the idea that it all ran in perfect working order like a clock. Each and every thing moving along in a predictable manner so that you could calculate events such as when the sun would rise, when an eclipse would happen and the journeys of the planets.

Deists (those that believe reason and observation of the natural world are sufficient to determine the existence of a Creator) latched onto the idea of the universe as a clock as proof that there was a god. If, they said, the universe is indeed as precise and predictable a machine as a clock, there must somewhere be a clockmaker and there must be someone who winds the mechanism to keep it going – and that person is God.

The Enlightenment was defined, by Immanuel Kant (see page 66), as man's release from immaturity; immaturity

Five Things You Didn't Know About Isaac Newton

1 It really was seeing an apple fall that led him to his gravitational theory

2. He was Master of the Royal Mint

3 He was MP for Cambridge University

4 In 1693 he suffered a nervous breakdown

5 He was born on Christmas Day, 1642

Something to Ponder

Newton said that each action has an equal opposite reaction. Think of various actions (a car moving, a ball falling, a dog standing up) and for each one decide what is the opposite reaction.

being an inability to act on one's own knowledge. So enlightenment is when your actions are dictated by what you know and have experienced, without having to refer to tradition or externally imposed edicts.

The Very Regular Immanuel Kant

Immanuel Kant was a man of habit; his daily activity was set out from when he woke at 5am until he retired late at night. If his routine ever varied it was such a shocking event that people in his home town of Königsberg in Prussia would rub their eyes in disbelief. Like the clockwork universe, his every move was regulated and his proud boast was that he never overslept. All of this tells us something of the man but does it tell us anything of his philosophy? 'Science is organised knowledge. Wisdom is organised life', he said.

His output of written work was quite phenomenal but he is best known for his *Critique of Pure Reason*. In this publication he attempts to understand the link between rationality and experience. He was convinced that our experiences are shaped by our mind – the upshot of which was that we do not experience things directly. So that when we touch something we do not experience how it feels immediately but via the mind.

Maybe this explains why Kant led such a structured life. Not for him the joy of smelling a rose during his morning walk. That would slow him down and would involve a major process of inputting the data (sniffing the rose), processing the information (allowing the sensation to wash around him) and coming to a conclusion (accepting that the rose smelt nice).

Critique of Pure Reason, published in 1781, ended an eleven-year gap in Kant's major published works, brought on by doubt about what he had said in his *Inaugural Dissertation*.

Did you know?

Something to Ponder

Can you think of anything that you have, or possibly could, experience without recourse to your senses?

Immanuel Kant

'All our knowledge begins with the senses, proceeds then to the understanding, and ends with reason. There is nothing higher than reason.'

Something Else to Ponder

Do you remember the diagram on page 59? How do you feel about the purple section now?

Jargon Buster

The Noumenal World The world that is experienced without the use of the senses. Kant said this may exist but was unknowable, as opposed to the phenomenal world which is experienced via the senses.

For Kant, space and time were subjective not objective categories

SPACE   TIME

Hegel Discovers History

Georg Wilhelm Friedrich Hegel (1770–1831) took up the baton where Kant left off but changed the emphasis to proceed from a logical point of view. The most important element of which was to put our understanding of behaviour into a historical context. In doing this he acknowledged the importance of tradition in shaping the way we are.

You can't, he argued, look at someone's behaviour without considering the context within which those actions took place. At a very simple level, if you saw a car driving on the right side of the road, you may think them insane, until you realise that this is the side they drive on in this country.

As a thinker who was happy to swim against the tide, he re-examined history from a teleological standpoint. The major result of this was that his writing was taken up by Karl Marx and formed the basis for what was to become communism.

Hegel's philosophy is summed up in, or labelled, *Absolute Idealism*. In order for a person to know the world he/she must be conscious of their own existence within that world, not just as being an individual within it, but in being a part of it.

Hegel saw human thought as constantly shifting between the eternal and the temporally specific. Philosophy therefore needed to take into account its own historical situation – 'We learn from history that we do not learn from history', he said. Moreover, Hegel

'Only one man ever understood me, and he didn't understand me.'

Georg Hegel

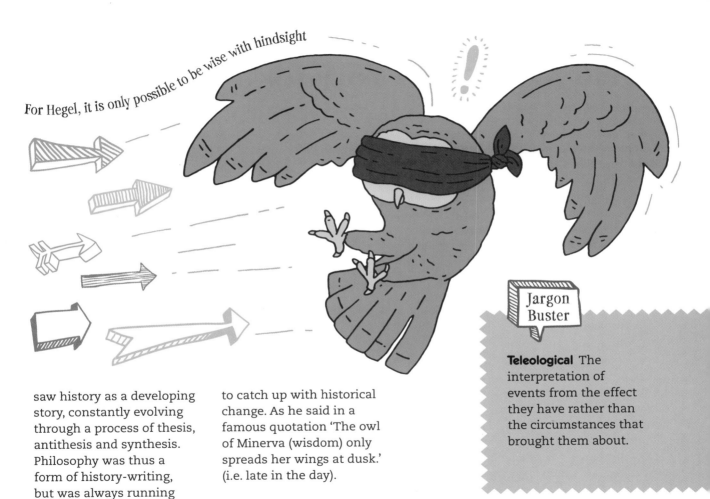

For Hegel, it is only possible to be wise with hindsight

Jargon Buster

Teleological The interpretation of events from the effect they have rather than the circumstances that brought them about.

saw history as a developing story, constantly evolving through a process of thesis, antithesis and synthesis. Philosophy was thus a form of history-writing, but was always running to catch up with historical change. As he said in a famous quotation 'The owl of Minerva (wisdom) only spreads her wings at dusk.' (i.e. late in the day).

Reality is Within You Jean-Jacques Rousseau and Romanticism

St Francis Xavier said 'Give me the child until he is seven and I will give you the man'. Jean-Jacques Rousseau's formative years are a classic proof of this assertion. His mother died while giving birth to him and his father had neither the time nor the desire to impose any discipline on the young boy. Growing up in rural Switzerland he loved nature and was allowed to run free without the usual hindrance of parental control.

If the age of Enlightenment gave a fresh new look at the power of reason, it was still held within limits. These boundaries were crashed through by the likes of Rousseau and his fellow romantics. There is a paragraph in his *Discourse on Inequality* (1755) which illustrates this perfectly. In it he says that all wars, crimes and horrors were the result of the first man putting up fences around a plot of land and claiming it to be his. All that was bad in the world could have been avoided, he suggests, if someone had pulled up

A true Romantic?

Jean-Jacques Rousseau

'The world of reality has its limits, the world of imagination is boundless.'

Something to Ponder
What would happen today if all forms of ownership were abandoned? Would the world be a better place? Would your life be better?

those fences and cried out '...you are undone if you once forget that the fruits of the earth belong to us all, and the earth itself to nobody.'

To the established society, this was a shocking suggestion, one which could lead to anarchy and Rousseau was condemned as a madman; in some ways you can see why when you remember the social contract. He felt that the best point in human development had been when man had been somewhere between an animal and the overly civilised individual that he witnessed in the 18th century.

The Romanticism that spread throughout Europe in the 18th century is often remembered for its liberal attitudes to life but probably one of its most long-lasting results was its impact on literature and art. It was hugely influential among writers and artists such as William Wordsworth, Joseph Turner and Franz Schubert.

Did you know?

Rousseau did not restrict himself to philosophy and was a renowned novelist and composer.

What is Art?

We've all *done* art at school, and when we do it, probably the first thing we do is painting or drawing. It isn't necessarily brilliant but it must be art simply because that's what the lesson is called but what, really, is art?

The classic definition would hold that it is work, produced using creativity and technique, of mainly a visual form, most usually painting or sculpture. A classic example of art is Leonardo Da Vinci's *Mona Lisa*, probably the most famous painting in the world. No one would argue that this is art but what about Marcel Duchamp's *L.H.O.O.Q*? This work was created by Duchamp by taking a cheap postcard of the *Mona Lisa* and drawing on it a moustache and beard and adding his title beneath it.

This piece fell into the category of what Duchamp referred to as *readymades*, where he took an everyday object and altered it, or in some cases did nothing to it, and then placed it in a gallery. His most famous *readymade* is *Fountain*, which is a standard urinal. The only change he made to it was to sign it with the pseudonym R Mutt.

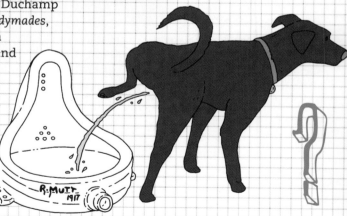

Had he simply placed this urinal in an unidentified toilet somewhere in Paris next to all the other urinals no one would have thought it was art, in fact they would have used it for what it was originally intended. Its function changed the moment he entered it for exhibition in the 1917 Society of Independent Artists. The committee rejected it but it is now recognised as one of the most important pieces of art of the 20th century. So art does not have to be a painting, or sculpture, it does not even have to have been produced, or maybe manufactured is a better word, by the artist who presents it.

In 1990 Charles Saatchi bought a piece by Damien Hirst entitled *A Thousand Years*. The work consisted of a decaying cow's head being consumed by flies and maggots. Not necessarily something you would want to put on your living room wall but certainly a conversation starter.

Maybe then the definition of art needs to be as vague as possible. Something along the lines of 'Something presented by someone which someone else thinks is art.'

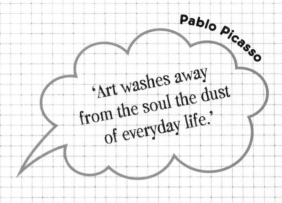

Pablo Picasso

'Art washes away from the soul the dust of everyday life.'

Something to Ponder

Can you come up with a perfect definition of art? Is beauty really in the mind of the beholder? If so, why do so many people find similar things beautiful?

Morals by Numbers
Bentham's Felicific Calculus

The Industrial Revolution, possibly more than any political revolution, changed the world beyond recognition and as a result changed our lives. The effects of it are still being felt now, all around the world, over 250 years after it all began. In many ways the move from agriculturally based society to industrial made life much better but there was much that was negative about it.

The new cities, and enlarged towns, that resulted from the mass migrations, created problems which had not been seen before. In Britain, where it all began, both the size of cities and the number of big industrial towns increased tenfold. By 1850s Britain, the number of people living in the metropolis was more than that living on the land, the first country in the world where this was the case. Over-crowding, poor housing, inadequate sanitation and generally short-sighted planning led to numerous problems.

Jeremy Bentham was a social reformer who identified these problems and wanted to do something about them. His philosophy was that of doing the most good for the most people. If you change something or impose a law it has to increase the overall happiness of the people. This philosophy is called *Utilitarianism* and the engine behind it, in Bentham's case, was his *felicific calculus*. This was an algorithm (step-by-step mathematical equation) whereby you could supposedly calculate if the decision you were making

would lead to an increase in the overall good, or at least a decrease in the negatives.

In Chapter 4 of his publication *An Introduction to the Principles of Morals and Legislation*, Bentham listed the inputs for his calculation…

Something Philosophical

'Create all the happiness you are able to create; remove all the misery you are able to remove.'
Bentham

Did you know?

When Bentham died, in 1832, he left his estate to University College London with one condition, that his body be wheeled into college board meetings. They embalmed it, and even now, he still attends.

'To a number of persons, with reference to each of whom to the value of a pleasure or a pain is considered, it will be greater or less, according to seven circumstances: to wit, the six preceding ones; viz.

1 Its intensity.	**2** Its duration.	**3** Its certainty or uncertainty.	**4** Its propinquity [proximity] or remoteness.
5 Its fecundity [reproductive rate].	**6** Its purity.	**7** Its extent; that is, the number of persons to whom it extends; or (in other words) who are affected by it.'	

And one other; to wit: ➡

The idea was to put all the data in one end and out the other would come the answer. Sadly it's not quite as simple as that but the principle is certainly there.

Mary Wollstonecraft
Women Are Equal but Not the Same

Mary Wollstonecraft died at the relatively young age, even for the 18th century, of 38 due to complications while giving birth to her second child. It is impossible to guess what her influence would have been had she lived longer, but her impact was still huge. In a world dominated by men it is not really a surprise that one of her main areas of philosophical interest was the equality of women.

She lived at a time (she was born in 1759) when a woman's place was still firmly felt to be in the home. The result of this was that educational opportunities for women were limited. Why educate someone in the classics, conventional wisdom held, when they will just be running the household? This created a vicious cycle in which women were seen as inferior, due to a lack of education, so had lesser ambitions and limited opportunities and thus seemingly proved those impressions correct.

Her best known work is *A Vindication of the Rights of Women* and it is here that she puts forward the arguments described above. She proposes that men and women are intellectually equal and,

Mary Wollstonecraft

'My own sex, I hope, will excuse me, if I treat them like rational creatures, instead of flattering their fascinating graces, and viewing them as if they were in a state of perpetual childhood, unable to stand alone.'

given the chance, women could prove this. The two sexes should be treated as equal according to their virtues, although she does concede that physically men are stronger. Her ideas on education build on the subject of her first publication, *Thoughts on the Education of Daughters*.

She took her passion for feminine advancement into her two novels: *Mary: A Fiction* and *Maria: or The Wrongs of Woman*. Both of these works of fiction see a wife wronged or put-down by her husband. The power granted a husband over his wife was something that Wollstonecraft fought against throughout her life.

It was not until the 20th century that women were granted equal rights anywhere in the world – some countries still do not allow it – but wherever equality exists there is little doubt that the root of it can be traced back to Wollstonecraft.

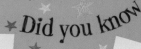

Finland was the first country to give all adults full suffrage, in 1906.

Did you know?

Really Free
John Stuart Mill's *On Liberty*

The idea that we should be striving to increase the overall good of society seems like a perfectly sensible, and just concept. John Stuart Mill, while still concerned with the overall feeling of wellbeing, directed his gaze at how this might affect an individual's freedom.

Did You Know?

Sitting as an MP for Westminster (1865–68), Mill was one of the first people to call for women to be given the right to vote.

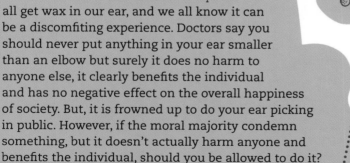

Did you hear about the accountant with too much earwax? He had to work it out with a pencil. We all get wax in our ear, and we all know it can be a discomfiting experience. Doctors say you should never put anything in your ear smaller than an elbow but surely it does no harm to anyone else, it clearly benefits the individual and has no negative effect on the overall happiness of society. But, it is frowned up to do your ear picking in public. However, if the moral majority condemn something, but it doesn't actually harm anyone and benefits the individual, should you be allowed to do it? Or more importantly, should society be allowed to stop you doing it? At worst it's a victimless crime.

Mill was very clear on this point:

'Mankind are greater gainers by suffering each other to live as seem good to themselves than by compelling each to live as seems good to the rest.'

The driving force behind Mill's philosophy was that personal freedom was an important driving factor in self-improvement and, if everyone improved themselves, society as a whole would benefit. Looking at it the other way, if you restrict freedom, you discourage self-improvement and society suffers.

Mill's father worked with Jeremy Bentham, who acted as tutor to the younger Mill. It is no surprise therefore that, like Bentham, Mill was a utilitarian, but their definition of happiness differed. For Bentham, happiness was an absolute and he did not account for qualitative differences. The amount of happiness was all that mattered. But for Mill, there was a qualitative element such that he disagreed with Bentham's assertion that 'push-pin is as good as poetry'.

I'M FREE TO DO WHAT I WANT!

JS Mill

'A person may cause evil to others not only by his actions but by his inaction, and in either case he is justly accountable to them for the injury.'

Something to Ponder
Can you think of some other 'victimless crimes'? Should they be allowed?

The Trolley Problem

Philippa Foot (1920–2010) is a British philosopher who developed a thought experiment that has become known as the trolley problem. It started out as a legal problem, whereby a judge is put under pressure to find someone, anyone, guilty of a crime, for which the real culprit is unknown. The pressure is coming from an angry mob, which is threatening to kill a section of the community if a scapegoat is not found. For the judge, the problem could be put quite simply: frame an innocent party (who would be put to death) or do nothing and a greater number of people will die.

Foot makes it more straightforward, and here is your problem…

A runaway train (or a trolley, as in the experiment's name) is hurtling towards five people tied to a track. You can save them by diverting the train on to another track on which is tied one person. You only have those choices: do nothing or do something.

A utilitarian, such as Bentham, would say you only have one option: kill the one, although they may not phrase it quite so callously. It seems obvious, and once you are aware of the situation can you really just walk away? But by shifting the train you become involved in the moral wrong that is already there. Perhaps by doing nothing you are not involved at all.

Not so simple.

Since Foot first came up with the trolley problem, further complications have been added, the first of which is known as The Fat Man. In this modification of the problem, the other track disappears but you get the option to throw a passing

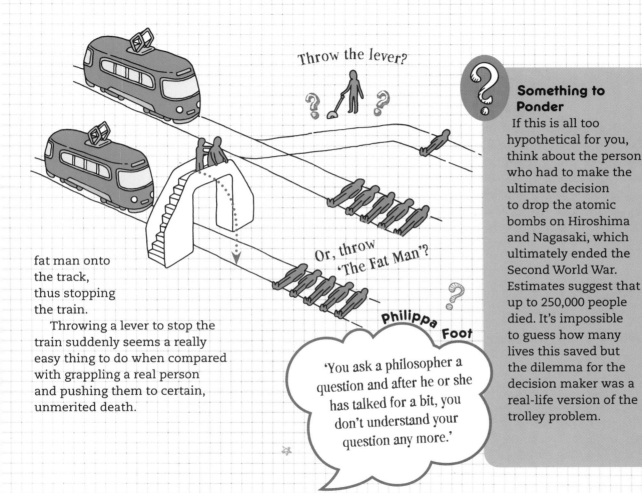

Throw the lever?

Or, throw 'The Fat Man'?

fat man onto the track, thus stopping the train.

Throwing a lever to stop the train suddenly seems a really easy thing to do when compared with grappling a real person and pushing them to certain, unmerited death.

Philippa Foot

'You ask a philosopher a question and after he or she has talked for a bit, you don't understand your question any more.'

Something to Ponder

If this is all too hypothetical for you, think about the person who had to make the ultimate decision to drop the atomic bombs on Hiroshima and Nagasaki, which ultimately ended the Second World War. Estimates suggest that up to 250,000 people died. It's impossible to guess how many lives this saved but the dilemma for the decision maker was a real-life version of the trolley problem.

Workers of the World Unite Karl Marx

Karl Marx studied philosophy and then law but it is his writings on communism for which he is best known. In his late teens Marx became interested in the work of the German idealist Hegel (see page 68) and was a member of a group known as The Young Hegelians. They didn't necessarily agree with everything Hegel said but they did utilise his dialectical methods to look at the world from a left-wing viewpoint: a view that placed emphasis on the condition of the working classes, rather than defending the status of the rich. While Marx's writings became more and more politicised, it did not mean that they became any less important in terms of their philosophical perspective.

In the same way that Bentham was determined to find a way to increase the lot of society as a whole, Marx felt that society, as it was in the mid-19th century, was geared towards exploiting the work of the many to advance the lot of the few. While this may increase the 'average wellbeing' of a country, for Marx it was at too great a cost to the working man, whose extra value was turned into profit for the factory owners.

Marx saw that a cycle had been forming and repeating where developments in methods of production improved the lot of the working man, and the owners, up to a point but then began to get in the way of human growth. As these cycles repeated, he believed that capitalism would collapse and communism would become the dominant world order to the betterment of mankind. He wasn't prepared to predict exactly how and when this would all resolve itself, just that eventually it would.

KARL MARX TIMELINE

Born
5 May 1818

Aged 6
Baptised

Aged 12
Enters Trier High School

Aged 17
Enrols Bonn University
– to study law

Aged 18
Changes to
Berlin University

Aged 22
Father
dies

Aged 25
Marries Jenny
von Westphalen

Aged 26
Daughter Jenny
Caroline born

Aged 26
Moves to
Paris

Aged 27
Daughter Jenny
Laura born

Aged 28
Moves to
Brussels

Aged 29
Son Edgar
born

Aged 31
Son Henry
born

Aged 31
Moves to
London

Aged 33
Daughter Jenny
Eveline born

Aged 37
Daughter Jenny
Julia born

Aged 39
A son is born
but dies before
being named

Aged 49
Das Kapital
(Vol.1)
published

Aged 64
Dies – Buried in
Highgate Cemetery,
North London

'The production of too many useful things results in too many useless people.'

'The philosophers have only *interpreted* the world, in various ways. The point, however, is to *change it*.'

'Workers of the world unite; you have nothing to lose but your chains.'

Karl Marx

The Will to Power Friedrich Nietzsche

Friedrich Nietzsche believed in the here and now, there was no world beyond and if you wanted to achieve anything it had to be during your life. This anti-Christian stance was termed *life-affirmation* and was discussed in his writings known as *The Will to Power*.

Friedrich Nietzsche

'If we affirm one moment, we thus affirm not only ourselves but all existence.'

The Will to Power [der Wille zur Macht] forms the foundation of Nietzsche's writings on why humans behave the way they do. He felt this was the main motivation for our actions, specifically ambition, the desire to reach the best place in life. About a hundred years after Nietzsche put this idea forward, Abraham Maslow came up with his Hierarchy of Needs, a sort of pyramid of achievement with physical needs at the base and the fulfilment of one's ambitions at the top.

With his life-affirmation Nietzsche was encouraging us to embrace and enjoy everything we experience, be it good or bad, because it had taken all eternity to produce that single moment. In affirming that moment then we were recognising and justifying the history of the world. To ignore that moment, any moment, would have been a crime as it would be denying our very existence. In some ways, then, he was going all the way back to Socrates.

Nietzsche wrote *Gott ist tot* (God is dead) in *The Gay Science* and in saying it he was trying to argue that the existing foundations of society were collapsing and that life was thus losing its meaning. The challenge in the face of this was to find out what your life was about.

One of Nietzsche's best known quotes is 'That which does not kill us makes us stronger', and so it is somewhat ironic that he died at the relatively young age of 55 after a prolonged illness.

Something to Ponder

There is only the moment, it is created by the billions of accumulated moments leading up to it but all we can actually do is live in the moment. The difficult thing is to identify and feel the moment, because once you start to think about it, that moment has gone and you're on to the next one. Try for a few minutes to genuinely live in the moment. Is it possible?

Believe What is Best
Pragmatism and the Secretive Squirrel of William James

The ability to believe in a god without having the evidence up front was, according to William James, not so different to having the confidence in one's self to achieve something without ever having accomplished that thing before. It seems obvious but it was all down to self-belief.

You may never have jumped across a stream before, indeed may never have jumped over anything, but there is nothing wrong with believing that you can do it and just going for it. In the same way, you can believe in a god in spite of a total lack of evidence because sometimes, as with the belief that you can jump a stream, you need to do it before you know you can do it. Without wishing to push the analogy too far, what is needed is a leap of faith.

Linked to James' *will to believe* was his pragmatic method. This was first discussed in a lecture from 1904 which begins with a story about a squirrel, a man and a tree.

James told of a time when he joined a discussion about whether a man chasing a squirrel around the trunk of a tree could be said to have 'gone around' the rodent, which keeps running around to the opposite side of the tree. The party had split into two equal groups, so it was James who would have the casting vote. His pragmatic method suggested that both sides were right, depending on the meaning of the phrase 'to go around'.

BOO!

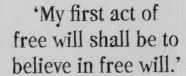

'My first act of free will shall be to believe in free will.'

One meaning is moving from a position facing the squirrel's back to facing his front. The other is moving to a geographical position to the north, east, south and west of him. As he explained: 'The pragmatic method in such cases is to try to interpret each notion by tracing its respective practical consequences. What difference would it practically make to anyone if this notion rather than that notion were true?'

James clearly liked the animal world as another of his better known theories, to do with emotions generally, and fear specifically, concerned how we react when we are confronted with a bear. The question he asks is: Do we run because we are afraid, or are we afraid because we run? The point he is making is about the nature of fear and how we recognise it as an emotion. The quickened heart rate and breathing, a pulsing in the brain, and so on. Do these come first, telling us we are afraid and so we run, or do we run on instinct, thus creating these physiological reactions which we recognise as fear?

Pacificism and Paradox
Bertrand Russell

Bertrand Russell was neither a barber nor the wearer of a beard so one of the most complex pieces of logic developed by him, or anyone else, may or may not be applied to him.

Think about a barber who shaves all those, and only those, men in the town who do not shave themselves. Does the barber therefore shave himself? If he shaves himself, then he can no longer be part of his customer group, but having stopped shaving himself he then becomes part of his customer group. A simple way out of this logical maze is to say the barber is a woman (although women do shave their legs) but you can see how your mind could be twisted.

Why is Russell's paradox important? It's all to do with mathematics. Russell's paradox highlights a problem with *naïve set theory* which forms part of the foundations of mathematics. In exposing this flaw, Russell established himself in one small stroke as a major mathematician and logician.

Russell suggests that mathematics, and logic, is important as far as philosophy is concerned because it allows for definite answers to be achieved, thus bringing stringency to the subject making it more of a science.

As well as his achievements in mathematics and philosophy, Russell is best known for his political activism, specifically his advocacy of pacifism. During World War One he was convicted under the Defence of the Realm Act. He continued to fight, maybe not the right word here, against war during World War Two and beyond. As he said, 'War does not determine who is right – only who is left.'

Bertrand Russell

'Mathematics, rightly viewed, possesses not only truth, but supreme beauty – a beauty cold and austere, like that of sculpture, without appeal to any part of our weaker nature, without the gorgeous trappings of painting or music, yet sublimely pure, and capable of a stern perfection such as only the greatest art can show.'

Something to Ponder

Can you think of another example of the application of Russell's Paradox? This may help you:

The ___er who only ___s those who don't ___ themselves.

Just fill in the gaps.

89

Wittgenstein Changes his Mind

For someone who is considered one of the most influential philosophers of the 20th century it is surprising to realise that, during his lifetime, Ludwig Wittgenstein only published one book on the subject. Published in 1921 *Tractatus Logico-Philosophicus* is just 75 pages long. Wittgenstein states that in it he intends to establish the link between language and reality. It was a demanding goal to set himself.

Wittgenstein and Adolf Hitler were born six days apart and went to the same school. They were not in the same class because Hitler was held back a year and Wittgenstein was pushed up a year.

Did you know?

A major step towards this goal is a leap back to the ancient Greeks' idea of atomism but taking it forward by creating *logical atomism*. So where the Greeks believed that everything was made up of atoms that could not be divided, Wittgenstein, among others, suggested that the world was made up of logical *atoms*, or facts, that could not be divided. It is worth noting that although it was actually Bertrand Russell who first used the phrase *logical atomism* he did so with clear thanks to Wittgenstein.

It was this book, and the theories in it, which put Wittgenstein at the forefront of philosophy but then, posthumously with the publication of *Philosophical Investigations*, he performed a total U-turn, and dismissed his own theory.

In the latter book he completely rejects his simplified version of the world as expressed with logical atomism, going as far as to say that it

Tractatus Logico-Philosophicus

Philosophical Investigations

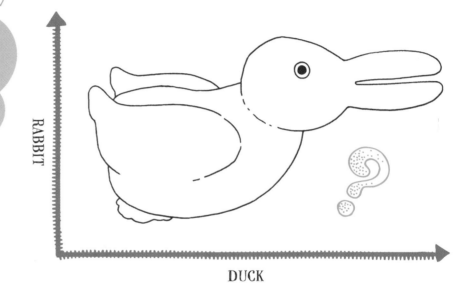

'The limits of my language are the limits of my mind. All I know is what I have words for.'

RABBIT

DUCK

would be a major error to view language as the same as logic. Instead he sees it from a more anthropological perspective (the study of humans), as linked to our behaviour, our habits and our form of life.

In the book Wittgenstein also discusses how we can initially see things one way but on further examination we can see them as something else – perhaps thus excusing his own

about-face. The example he uses is the duckrabbit. This is a drawing which, on first glance, looks like a duck, but when studied for longer suddenly resembles

a rabbit. He describes the differences in these two interpretations of the same image as seeing that it's a rabbit, versus seeing it as a duck.

The Beetle in a Box

Wittgenstein developed an interesting analogy for the relationship between our language and our mental states. What, he suggested, if everyone had a small box in which they kept a beetle. The only person who can look at your beetle is you but you are allowed to talk about your beetle and discuss it with other people, they just cannot ever actually look inside the box and see it.

What he was highlighting is that meaning and description develops through public usage and agreement. So, while you can describe what your beetle looks like, it is only through a process of

agreement of terms that your description can be understood. With the beetle this is quite straightforward but still fraught with difficulties, so that when you then translate this to discussing your mind it quickly becomes apparent that it is close to impossible ever to truly understand someone else's mind.

We all have boxes (our heads, or brains, depending on where you think the

mind is stored) and some are bigger than others. We are free, and often encouraged, to discuss our box and its contents with other people, but it is impossible to see what is really in someone else's box. Even if someone gives a really accurate description of their mind, you still cannot be sure that it is correct. After all, what is real and true to you about your box's contents may well not be

'Philosophy is a battle against the bewitchment of our intelligence by language.'

Ludwig Wittgenstein

Something to Ponder
The beetle in the box forms part of Wittgenstein's *private language argument*. A private language, ie one that is only understandable to an individual, is of no value and is, in a sense, impossible because it does not allow for communication except with oneself.

the same for someone else. One person's depression, for instance, might equate to another's euphoria.

It's also worth considering that it might actually be easier to describe your beetle than your mind. Is it possible for something to genuinely, objectively, describe itself?

One of the important points about this analogy is that while we generally believe that people's minds work in the same way, thinking about the beetle we can see that they could potentially be very different. It is also interesting to note that while we refer to it as 'the mind' (or the beetle), what we are really saying is 'that which is in the box' because we cannot ever know what someone else refers to when they talk about their mind. On a very simplistic level, what you call a beetle might not even be what I call a beetle. If you could look inside my box you might find that I've actually got a ladybird.

Being and Time
Heidegger and the Philosophy of the Forest

In his book *Being and Time* (1927), Martin Heidegger creates a notional being, Dasein, as the fundamental concept from whose perspective the world is seen. Dasein is German for *existence*, or *presence*, perhaps most closely translated as *being there*. Maybe it should be *being here* because one of the central cores of Heidegger's philosophy, or discussions on philosophy, is that philosophers before him had stopped asking what being was.

What he was trying to say was that we had forgotten about actually being, that of ourselves and objects, and only looked at things for what they could do. The example he gave was a hammer. All we cared about, or thought about, was the hammer's ability to knock nails in, we did not think about the hammer actually being there. He felt this extended to everything including ourselves.

Accepting this is the first part of Heidegger's insight, the second part is to do with caring. We have to ask the question about being but it has to be asked by a person who cares about it, or for whom being matters. It is this person that Heidegger refers to as Dasein and about whom, or from whose perspective *Being and Time*, Heidegger's first published work, is written.

Heidegger did most of his writing in a small cabin in the Black Forest. *Die Hütte* was his place to be but it is not recorded as to whether he just saw it as a place to write or appreciated itself for its being. Let's be generous and say he probably did.

95

What is it Like to Be a Bat?

Reductionism, in philosophy, implies that any complex system can be reduced to its individual parts. It is from Thomas Nagel's rejection of reductionism that he came up with his discussion of what it is like to be a bat.

The point of his essay is to refine our understanding of consciousness by showing what it is like to be that creature. That all animals possess a conscious mind and that all it needs for this to be the case is that it has something special about it, where *something special* is that thing which makes it it.

So while we can imagine doing some bat-like things such as flying or swinging upside down from a branch, we can only imagine what these would be like from our human perspective. Thus, when we imagine them we are not imagining being a bat and feeling the feelings and having the thoughts that a bat would have. All we are doing is imagining what it would be like for a human to hang upside down.

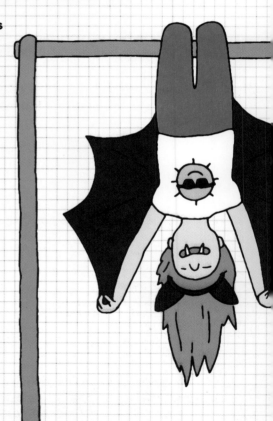

Something to Ponder

Before reading on, try it now. Imagine being a bat. What is the first thing you think of?

Most people, when they imagine hanging upside down, would instinctively have a human response to it. This is not a criticism of your imagination, just a realisation of the hard-wired nature of your mindset. When you first imagine hanging upside down, you are probably worried about things falling out of your pockets, or the pain you will get in your knees from holding yourself up. These are both things that would happen to you but they wouldn't happen to a bat. Bats don't have pockets and they don't hang by way of bending their knees around a branch. You see instantly then how hard it is to get out of your mindset and it is now a long way back to get into the mind of the bat. So far, in fact, that it is not possible and that is before we even consider bats' incredible method of navigation by sonar.

Something Else to Ponder

So now having worked out the problems of thinking like a bat do you think you can do it? Would a bat be able to imagine what it's like being a human?

Science is Only Good at Being Wrong
Karl Popper's Falsificationism

Karl Popper (1902–1994) said that science did not arrive at truth and what made science *science* was that it put forward theories that were capable of being falsified. By falsified, he did not necessarily mean that they were wrong, because at the time they were put forward they probably appeared correct. What he was highlighting was that by putting forward falsifiable theories we were, or rather scientists were, showing that science is defined by its method, rather than simply what it discovers.

Did you know?

Popper was born in Austria but spent many years trying to leave to avoid the rise of the right-wing rulers. The experiences of his youth and early adulthood formed the backbone of his political thinking.

It may be that truth is never reached but as a theory is falsified we move further along the path, a path that is only made possible by laying ourselves open to being proved wrong. He celebrated the bravery of such scientists in being prepared to put their necks on the block for such treatment:

'...every time we succeed in falsifying a theory of this kind, we make an important new discovery. For these falsifications are most important. They teach us the unexpected...'

Karl Popper

'Our knowledge can only be finite, while our ignorance must necessarily be infinite.'

A better way to understand what Popper meant by *falsifiability* is to ask the question: Can this statement, or theory, be falsified? For example, going back to our old friends the white swans (see page 62), the statement *all swans are white* can, logically, be falsified by observing a black swan.

Why was falsifiability important to Popper? For him it was vital to be able to distinguish between what is science and what is not and it is the falsifiability of something that marked the line, thus if something could not be falsified, he would say it was not science. Wolfgang Pauli even stated of theories that cannot be falsified that:

'This isn't right. This isn't even wrong.'

Something to Ponder
Consider some of the great scientific discoveries and ask yourself are they falsifiable? Here's a starter – gravity.

Can a Machine Think?

In fiction it is often taken for granted that there will be a time when machines can think for themselves. A prime example is the *Terminator* series, which hit the screens in 1984 but is set in 2029. If we are to realise this particular dream, or nightmare, we do not have long to go and we really need to pass The Turing Test pretty quickly.

The Turing Test was an experiment proposed by the father of modern computing, Alan Turing. He suggested that the way to test if a computer could think like a human would be for someone to have a conversation with a computer and a human and not be able to tell which was which. Anyone who has had to deal with an automated telephone receptionist will realise this is a long way off

but Turing was optimistic that it could happen.

'It seems probable,' he said, 'that once the machine thinking method had started, it would not take long to outstrip our feeble powers… They would be able to converse with each other to sharpen their wits. At some stage therefore, we should have to expect the machines to take control.'

We know already that

it is quite simple for a machine to answer factual questions such as what day is it, or how many pigs of size X can I fit in a pen of size Y? But for the machine to convince us that it is human it needs to go beyond this. It would need to be able to go beyond calculating, as in the examples above, and into the realm of genuinely thinking and having opinions. At present, even

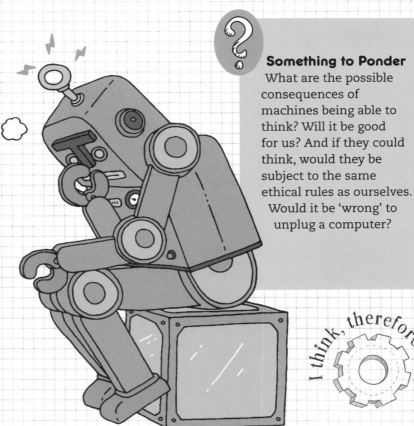

now more than 60 years after Turing, computers are only as good as the people who programmed them. What goes in, is pretty much what comes out. The giant leap forward will be when someone creates a machine that can actually learn, that can learn things we have not already put into it.

Something to Ponder

What are the possible consequences of machines being able to think? Will it be good for us? And if they could think, would they be subject to the same ethical rules as ourselves. Would it be 'wrong' to unplug a computer?

I think, therefore I am?

Crazy Science Thomas Kuhn and Copernicus's Leap in the Dark

The paradigm shift is not a fancy type of dress worn by scientists' wives but is instead a leap or jump away from the norm. It's a jump so unexpected that it is the equivalent of a train jumping tracks and taking its passengers off in a whole new direction.

What makes the change so amazing is that the new tracks are ones that could not even be conceived within the passengers' current understanding of the existing train network.

Such a shift was that of Nicolaus Copernicus when he established that the planets in our solar system move around the Sun and not around the Earth in the 16th century.

It was such a gigantic scientific leap that he dared not publish his findings publicly and only let a few of his closest friends and colleagues know for fear of the repercussions.

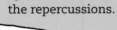

'Normal science, the activity in which most scientists inevitably spend almost all their time, is predicated on the assumption that the scientific community knows what the world is like.'

Thomas Kuhn

Did you know?

Do you remember Wittgenstein's duckrabbit? Well, Kuhn used the same idea when trying to illustrate the concept of the paradigm shift.

Copernicus' leap is an example given by Thomas Kuhn in trying to explain that science does not move in a straight line, with each new discovery leading inevitably on to the next. Rather, he suggests, every now and then there is a leap into the dark.

Kuhn described the cycle of scientific progress in three main stages. Starting with *pre-science*, where insufficient is known about the topic to move it forward. This is followed by *normal science*, where the bulk of the work and advancements are made. It is during this phase that ideas from an opposing paradigm are ignored as being so off-piste as to be wrong, dangerous or just plain silly. Finally, there is the *revolutionary science* where anomalies in the existing paradigm build up to such an extent that a shift has to occur to allow further advancement.

Many have argued that simply by identifying this cycle Kuhn has allowed science to move forward quicker. By giving scientists *permission* to go off on a tangent, they feel less inclined to stick within the existing paradigm for as long as they might otherwise. Had Copernicus been given such a shove history could well have been different.

Do Animals Have Rights?

In the animal world, away from the sight of humans, animals treat each other in a way that we might find intolerable. They hunt each other down and kill one another. There is no consideration for the rights of the hunted. There is not a second thought for whether the prey's final moments are distressful. What is happening is natural. The food chain has to be linked for the good of the whole planet.

No one would argue with the way in which the world in the wild runs but if we now impose our human morals on to this natural world, it wouldn't work. The lion could no more kill an antelope *humanely* than it could juggle tennis balls. This seems right and proper and yet we, the humans, supposedly at the top of the food chain, have spent millennia considering the rights of animals. Is it the right of an animal that we breed for our food to be treated well? Does it make any difference to a chicken, whose destiny is to be sold for food, whether it spends its short life in an open field with space to roam or in a cage where it can't even turn around? Because we have developed rights for each other and rules for our behaviour towards other humans the debate now rages as to whether we should extend the same rights and considerations to non-humans, the animals.

The debate revolves around how and what animals actually think and feel, and how we, humans, feel about ourselves and how that feeling changes depending on how we treat others.

ORDER!

ORDER!

We wouldn't, we hope, lock up another human in a small cage for 18 months, with no natural light, force feeding him or her to fatten them up. So why is this done to chickens? Some would say we are not a source for our own food so we treat one another differently to all other animals on the planet.

When it comes down to it, we are meat eaters and we will find ways to produce and eat meat. There is no getting away from the fact that this will involve killing another animal. Is this whole argument just a way to prove that, while we accept our dietary needs, we have a need also to prove our superiority to the rest of the animal world not just by mastering them but by treating them better than they treat each other?

Peter Singer

'If possessing a higher degree of intelligence does not entitle one human to use another for his or her own ends, how can it entitle humans to exploit non-humans?'

Zombie Philosophy
The Problem of Other Minds

The zombies in philosophy are not the same as the zombies in the movies. It is difficult to force yourself away from the vision of the stumbling, dead eyed, arms-outstretched version but if you can it is a useful philosophical exercise.

David Chalmers

'Studying consciousness tells us more about how the world is fundamentally strange. I think we have a few revolutions to go yet before we get to the bottom of it.'

In philosophy, the zombie is just like you and me except it has no consciousness. It is, in essence, a blank human. These zombies have been created by philosophers such as David Chalmers, to counter the arguments of physicalism. Philosophical zombies are hypothetical beings that are physically identical to human beings but lack consciousness – there is therefore nothing that it is 'like' to be a zombie. If we can imagine this kind of zombie, Chalmers argues, then this reveals something about our

understanding of the mind and consciousness. For if we can imagine a being with our physical makeup but without the consciousness that accompanies it, it shows that physicalism is not true: for under physicalism the same physical conditions would be accompanied by the same mental events (as they are effectively physical).

The counter argument is that such zombies could not exist and are impossible to imagine: the same physical makeup would produce the same mental events. Such zombies would necessarily be as conscious as we are.

This counter argument raises another interesting area of thought. Just because we can imagine

Jargon Buster

Physicalism Everything is physical, there is nothing over and above the physical.

that, logically, something is possible, does that actually make it possible? Take for instance a golfer. He's on the last hole of the day and his round has taken a lot longer than he expected, so it is now dark and he can't even see the green, never mind the hole. Is it logically possible for him to be able to hit the ball

straight into the hole from 200 yards away? Logically yes, of course it's possible. Is it actually possible? Of course it is, even if not likely. The logic of the existence of the philosophy zombie is not so straightforward and hence the lack of agreement as to whether the logic could be translated to the real world.

The Future of Philosophy

As technology strides forward, the pace of change and advancement in science increases exponentially. Each new invention and discovery means that the next one comes along in a shorter time. Our world is getting smaller and smaller every day. We can travel a distance in a hundred minutes now that a hundred years ago would have taken ten times longer. We can speak face to face with someone on the other side of the planet with a device the size of our hand. Our world is changing so quickly now that it is difficult to know if our understanding of it can keep pace.

This question – are our lives altering too quickly for us to appreciate it? – is one that philosophers must address. As our world changes, our place in it changes and the things that were once important may no longer be so. The Earth's natural resources are dwindling at an ever increasing pace; when they run out, as surely they must, how will we cope? Not just cope in terms of powering our cars, and keeping a warm roof over our heads but how will society cope when a world powered by fossil fuels no longer has any fossil fuels?

If the petrol stations run dry, travel will be more difficult, prices will go up and products which are now staples will become luxuries. Will people still be prepared to sign up to the social contract when simply feeding ourselves

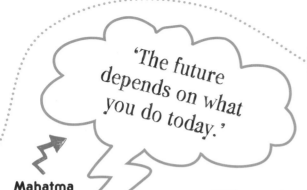

'The future depends on what you do today.'

Mahatma Ghandi

is our main daily activity? Will philosophy come to the fore to help us handle these changes, or will it be a discipline that falls away? A new Dark Age!

As diversity becomes the norm and we move further away from the traditional family unit, how will society change? With first-world countries suffering economic crises, will the shift of populations change how we live together?

Will computers finally become intelligent? Will they be able to think for themselves and, if they do, what will their opinion be of us and how we have treated the planet? Can an intelligent, thinking computer philosophise and if it can, what will it think of previous doctrines?

And maybe the biggest question of them all: In this vast universe, is it really possible that there are no other intelligent beings? We may only just now be coming to terms with our

place in this world but how will we cope if we have to think of ourselves in relation to other, perhaps more advanced, species? What would we do if we were no longer at the top of the food chain? Would it reveal that consciousness is not something that is or is not possessed, but is possessed in degrees?

Something to Ponder

You decide.

109

Glossary

Artificial intelligence
The field of philosophy and computer science that examines whether computers can exhibit intelligence equal or superior to human beings.

Atheism
The disbelief in the existence of God or gods.

Atomism
The idea that the world is composed of minute unchangeable particles, too small to be seen.

Axiom
In logic, a first principle taken to be absolutely true.

Communism
The political doctrine that holds all property in public ownership, a system established in Russia after the Revolution of 1917.

Dasein
'Existence', or 'being-there' – the characteristic mode of what it is to be a human being and the fundamental philosophical principle of Heidegger's *Being and Time* (1927).

Deduction
A process of reasoning from which a specific conclusion follows necessarily from certain premises: e.g., All men are mortal. Socrates is a man. Therefore Socrates is mortal.

Deism
The belief that the scientific investigation of the natural world reveals evidence for the existence of God.

Determinism
The theory that every event is the product of previous causes that could cause no other event.

Dualism
The belief that the universe is composed of two distinct and irreducible substances: mind and matter. It stands in contrast to Monism.

Empiricism
A method of enquiry, fundamentally associated with science, in which true knowledge can only be arrived at via the evidence of the senses.

Epistemology
The branch of philosophy which is concerned with the nature and availability and reliability of knowledge.

Ethics
The field of philosophy concerned with questions of moral principle – for example, whether suicide is ever morally acceptable.

Feminism
An ethical, social and intellectual movement that advocates women's rights on the grounds of the equality of the sexes.

Humanism
The branch of Renaissance thinking preoccupied with the literature and culture of the Greek and Roman worlds. More recently used to describe a non-religious or secular viewpoint.

Idealism
The belief that reality is necessarily the construct of the mind or consciousness and that no knowledge outside the mind or consciousness is therefore possible.

Induction
The process of arriving at general conclusions from specific premises: e.g.,

My brother likes pizza. Your brother likes pizza. Therefore, all brothers like pizza.

Metaphysics
The branch of philosophy that deals with the fundamental nature of reality, such as the nature of time, being and causation.

Monism
The belief that the universe is composed of one single, irreducible substance. It stands in contrast to Dualism.

Ontology
The section of metaphysics associated with the nature of being and existence, and such questions as: 'What exists?', and, 'Into what categories can we place the things that exist?'

Physicalism
In the philosophy of mind, the belief that all mental states are in fact physical states: that thought is ultimately reducible to matter.

Pragmatism
A brand of philosophy emerging in America in the late 19th century that held that decisions between opposing philosophical viewpoints should be settled in relation to the 'practical differences' that ensued from that decision.

Rationalism
In the history of philosophy, the strain of thinking that sees Reason as the true source of knowledge, and able to grasp truths beyond the evidence of the senses.

Scepticism
The philosophical position that knowledge is uncertain or ultimately unattainable.

Stoicism
A school of philosophy associated with the Greeks and Romans that argues that one achieves wisdom through a cultivated indifference to misfortune and physical pain.

Syllogism
In logic, an argument in which a conclusion is supported by a major premise and a minor premise, each of which has one term in common with the conclusion.

Teleology
From the Greek meaning 'purpose' or 'end'; the belief that historical events are best understood not in terms of their causes but in terms of an ultimate design or purpose.

Utilitarianism
A 19th century philosophy that analysed ethical decisions in terms of their impact upon the well-being of the majority – in Jeremy Bentham's phrase: 'the greatest happiness of the greatest number'.

Verificationism
An early 20th century school of philosophy that held that only statements that are in principle empirically verifiable have meaning. Hence some verificationists would argue that religious, ethical, and aesthetic statements are strictly speaking meaningless.

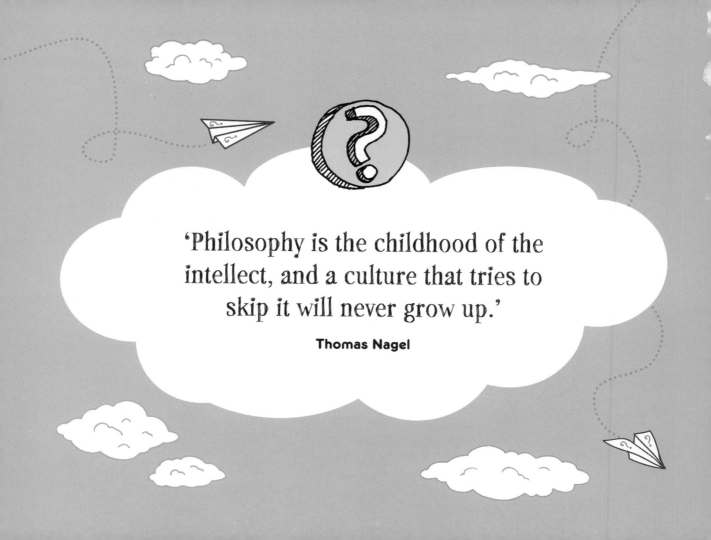

'Philosophy is the childhood of the intellect, and a culture that tries to skip it will never grow up.'

Thomas Nagel